SUPERCUT

SUPERCUT
NUTRITION FOR THE ULTIMATE PHYSIQUE

BILL REYNOLDS,
Editor-in-Chief, Muscle & Fitness

JOYCE L. VEDRAL, Ph.D.

CONTEMPORARY
BOOKS, INC.
CHICAGO

Library of Congress Cataloging in Publication Data

Reynolds, Bill.
  Supercut: nutrition for the ultimate physique.

  Includes index.
  1. Bodybuilders—Nutrition.   I. Vedral, Joyce L.
II. Title.
TX361.B64R49   1985   646.7'5   84-28510
ISBN 0-8092-5326-7

Special thanks to Joe Weider for use of photographs (photos of Dr. Joyce Vedral by Bill Reynolds).

Recipe calculations of calories, grams, protein, carbohydrate, and fat were done by Dr. Shelly Rothman, Associate Professor of Mathematics, Long Island University, C. W. Post Center. The book he used is: *Nutrition Almanac, Revised Edition*, McGraw-Hill Book Company, 1979.

Published by Contemporary Books, Inc.
180 North Michigan Avenue, Chicago, Illinois 60601
Manufactured in the United States of America
Library of Congress Catalog Card Number: 84-28510
International Standard Book Number: 0-8092-5387-9

Published simultaneously in Canada by Beaverbooks, Ltd.
195 Allstate Parkway, Valleywood Business Park
Markham, Ontario L3R 4T8 Canada

CONTENTS

Dawn Marie Gnaegi.

Lee Haney.

FOREWORD

You can hardly take our word for it that this guide to nutrition for bodybuilders is one of the most important investments you could have made. Therefore, we have asked two bodybuilders—a woman and a man—and a highly regarded authority on bodybuilding to provide their comments on our manuscript.

DAWN MARIE GNAEGI
UNITED STATES MIDDLEWEIGHT CHAMPION
(1984)

At 5′1″ in height, I once weighed 170 pounds, a majority of the weight situated between my waist and my knees. Today I compete weighing a muscular 115 pounds. As you might conclude, I am a firm believer in the important role diet plays in the complete bodybuilding process. I believe that you are what you eat, so you might as well eat in as healthy and appealing a manner as humanly possible.

Dieting for a competition should be interesting, not boring. More than 200 low-calorie recipes and a wide variety of sample meal plans are included in Bill Reynolds' and Joyce Vedral's *Supercut*, all of which will contribute to the variety and interest level of your next precontest diet. And the numerous dietary tips and strategies outlined in this book will make your next diet more effective than the last.

Meals that look good, taste good, and are as enjoyable to prepare as to eat can be prepared during both off-season and precontest cycles. I personally love to cook visually appealing food because it tastes better if it looks good. Using the philosophies and recipes in *Supercut* will allow you to cook the same way I do and experience the same results that I do on a precontest diet.

Good luck with your next diet. It won't be a completely easy process, but it will work wonders in changing the appearance of your physique!

LEE HANEY
AMERICAN CHAMPION, WORLD CHAMPION, NIGHT-OF-THE-CHAMPIONS WINNER, CESAR'S PALACE PRO INVITATIONAL CHAMPION, FIRST PLACE/1984 MR. OLYMPIA

Until the publication of Bill Reynolds' and Joyce Vedral's book, *Supercut,* there really wasn't an acceptable source of comprehensive information about the dietary process in bodybuilding. As a result, my own knowledge of bodybuilding diet came slowly and primarily through trial and error. I can honestly tell you that I would have become a champion at least a year sooner if I had had *Supercut* as a reference book when I started pumping iron.

Like most bodybuilders, I feel that a proper approach to nutrition is of paramount importance. During an off-season, mass-building cycle, I feel that it's at least 50 percent of the battle, with high-intensity training making up the other 50 percent. And as a competition grows close, the value of proper diet goes up. Just prior to a competition, my success potential comes at least 75 percent from correct diet and less than 25 percent from training. So if you understand how to diet correctly—and you have all of the right recipes and meal plans close at hand—you have a leg up on your opponents at every competition you enter.

I also feel that the dietary advice presented in *Supercut* is of benefit to athletes and appearance-minded individuals who need to lose body fat or put on muscular body weight. Bodybuilders, as a group, know more about nutrition than any other class of athlete, and our knowledge of proper eating can benefit almost everyone in our society.

Most of all, I feel that *Supercut* will benefit younger guys who don't have a wife who can cook up a storm, as my own wife, Shirley, does. If you've been eating plain old water-packed tuna right out of the can, you can use the information and recipes in *Supercut* to eat like a bodybuilding gourmet.

Bon appetit!

FREDERICK C. HATFIELD, PhD.
EDITOR-IN-CHIEF, *SPORTS FITNESS*

While nutrition is an infant science, there is no place on Earth where it has reached the heights of sophistication that it has in the sport of bodybuilding. While the average American remains overweight from overindulging in food and from inactivity, the men and women who ascribe to a bodybuilding lifestyle eat better and smarter, look better, feel better, and—by all standards—outperform the out-of-shape at their daily jobs. It's no accident that this difference exists, for while nutritionists worry about feeding poor folk and the "average" man and woman, bodybuilders have taken nutrition a giant step further—eating for peak athletic performance and maximum muscularity.

Bill Reynolds knows every major bodybuilding competitor in the entire world on a personal basis. He trains with them, he writes about them in *Muscle & Fitness* (for which he serves as editor-in-chief), and he knows what they eat and why. His practical knowledge of bodybuilding nutrition, coupled with the bodybuilding expertise of Dr. Joyce Vedral, makes *Supercut* state-of-the-art in every detail.

The main emphasis of this book is how to lose fat and how to keep it off. The low-fat/low-calorie dieting tips are complete, carefully thought out, and designed to maintain a high level of nutrition at the same time. Low-carbohydrate dieting is also discussed in practical and scientific terms.

For those who feel the need to put on some extra weight, *Supercut* describes exactly how it should be done—without putting on fat. Bodybuilders need to know how to cycle their diets in order to maximize their muscularity at contest time without reducing the nutritional value of each meal. The procedure involves the wise use of food supplements such as protein, vitamins, minerals, and trace elements as well as salt (sodium) and various enzymes for more complete and speedy digestion. All of these significant points are discussed thoroughly in this book.

Reynolds and Vedral have also amassed more than 200 low-calorie recipes that are favorites of top bodybuilders. Suggested meal plans accompany these recipes for more accurate planning of nutritional needs and caloric intake. Additionally, the favorite recipes of famous bodybuilders (such as Mohamed Makkawy, Tom Platz, Samir Bannout, Bill Pearl, and Candy Csencsits) are highlighted, as are meal plans from several of these international stars.

The book is virtually complete. There is a discussion on vegetarian diet plans (the problems and the alternatives) as well as information on how to stock a kitchen, how to cook—everything, in fact, except *how* to eat. And I rather suspect you'll have little problem with that after reading *Supercut*.

1
INTRODUCTION TO BODYBUILDING NUTRITION

As it relates to bodybuilding and sport in general, nutrition has been an inexact folk art for more than 2,500 years and a relatively exact science only during the past decade or two. And it's interesting to note that proper nutrition has been considered an aid to athletic performance for nearly 3,000 years, at least since the first recorded classic Olympic Games in 776 B.C.

Primitive societies have long consumed selected animal organs in an effort to improve specific valuable personal qualities. For example, they would eat the heart of a lion to improve their own courage and fortitude, or they would consume the lungs of a deer to increase their running speed and endurance.

The trainers of ancient Greek athletes discovered that they could increase the strength of their charges by regularly feeding them bull testicles. Even today, a host of food supplement distributors will seek to sell you raw orchis (desiccated bull testicle) tablets as a means of improving your own strength and muscular development. They'll also sell you raw heart, pancreas, liver, thyroid, and many other pills formed from animal organs.

Just as the public is prone to follow fad diets, bodybuilders have a history of adhering to various nutritional fetishes. During the 1930s and 1940s, for example, milk was considered to be a key bodybuilding food. The pages of muscle magazines of that period abounded with photos

1

of superstars like John C. Grimek, Jack Dellinger, and Steve Reeves quaffing huge bottles of moo juice.

Other popular bodybuilding foods during various eras have included fertile eggs; plain old eggs, but up to 50 of them per day; huge quantities of beef, both cooked and raw; beef liver; brewer's yeast; honey; desiccated liver; large quantities of powdered protein supplements; wheat germ oil; megadoses of vitamins and minerals; foods only from vegetarian sources; and many other foods and fads.

One area of bodybuilding nutrition in which fads have ebbed and flowed over the years is in the type of precontest diet followed by bodybuilders. And the relative severity of precontest diets has increased steadily—particularly in recent years—as a greater and greater accent has been placed on muscularity (lack of body fat) than on raw muscle mass (size).

Women didn't begin competing regularly in bodybuilding shows until 1979, so the early history of precontest dieting strictly involved only male bodybuilders. During the late 1940s and early 1950s, the accent in bodybuilding judging was primarily on muscle mass, with little attention paid to muscularity. A bodybuilder who wanted to harden up a little in those days would simply cut back a bit on his consumption of all foods, a crude but effective form of low-calorie dieting.

Since about 1960, there has been an increasing emphasis on muscularity, as well as on muscle mass, balanced physical proportions, and aesthetic symmetry (body shape). This trend probably reached its first big peak with Frank Zane's three consecutive Mr. Olympia victories from 1977 through 1979. It continues unabated to this day.

As bodybuilders were forced to become more and more muscular in order to keep up with the competition, they at first followed primarily a low-carbohydrate/high-fat/high-protein diet. This diet was effective but had severe drawbacks in terms of health maintenance. And while a low-carbohydrate diet stripped away body fat, most bodybuilders found it impossible to retain maximum muscle mass while on a low-carb regimen.

Beginning in about 1975, competitive bodybuilders increasingly turned to a more sensible, healthy, and effective low-fat/low-calorie diet. To the best of our knowledge, the first major bodybuilder to publicly acknowledge use of this diet was Rod Koontz (Mr. USA, Natural Mr. America). Today, the vast majority of all male and female competitive bodybuilders count calories in order to achieve peak muscularity for an important competition.

BODYBUILDING DIETARY CYCLES

Realizing that there are a significant number of exceptions to the rule, most bodybuilders follow a radically different diet during the off-season when attempting to increase muscle mass than prior to a show when trying to peak out. This off-season diet is explained in detail in Chapter 4, while the precontest diet is discussed in Chapter 3.

During the early stages of your involvment in bodybuilding, you will be on one long mass-building, off-season diet. It takes at least one or two years on this type of diet to build sufficient muscle mass to compete successfully. And after your first competition, you will alternate off-season and precontest dietary cycles as detailed in Chapter 5.

Prior to your first bodybuilding competition, it's a good idea to make dry runs with various diets, each lasting several weeks, in order to determine how well and how quickly your body reacts to each diet. This preliminary data will allow you to peak out optimally and at the correct time for a major show.

A WORD TO NONBODYBUILDERS

The average person can successfully use a bodybuilding diet to gain body weight or reduce body fat stores at will. While most people seem to be preoccupied with losing weight, there are large numbers of underweight men and women who would benefit from gaining a few pounds of well-distributed body weight. The diet outlined in Chapter 4—particularly when combined with a sensible weight training program—will help you add good-quality weight to your body if you need to gain weight.

Those men and women who desire to lose body fat and keep it off can do so quite effectively by following the low-fat/low-calorie diet described in Chapter 3 and culminated in the wide variety of recipes and meal plans in Chapters 7–15. There are no fads here, and we can't promise that you'll lose 10 pounds in two weeks, but a sensible bodybuilding-style diet will slowly peel off the pounds and keep them off!

CONSISTENCY

Ultimately, the effectiveness of any diet is a function of how consistently you follow it. To bodybuilders and appearance-minded individuals alike, diet is at least 50 percent of the battle in gaining or losing weight. And you'll get optimum results only if you're 100 percent consistent in applying the diet you have chosen to follow. Don't beat yourself. Eat like you're already a Miss Olympia or Mr. Olympia winner!

2
COOKING? THERE'S REALLY NOTHING TO IT

Many readers undoubtedly know how to cook, so this chapter is dedicated to those who are still eating water-packed tuna right out of the can. It's really not that difficult to prepare delicious and nutritious meals, and with only a little effort and experience you will soon be a bodybuilding gourmet cook.

The more than 200 recipes included in Chapters 7 through 13 have been carefully chosen for nutritional value, taste, visual appeal, and ease of preparation. We began with approximately 700 recipes and gradually eliminated those that failed to meet the foregoing criteria, until the 200 best recipes remained.

For your convenience when following a bodybuilding diet, we have listed the number of calories, grams of protein, grams of fat, and grams of carbohydrate per serving of every recipe in this book, including the recipes of leading bodybuilders included in Chapter 14.

Recipes are divided into seven chapters: Vegetable Dishes; Salads; Poultry and Dairy Dishes; Fish; Meat; Rice, Potato, and Grain Dishes; and Desserts. Using these recipes, you can select those that most appeal to you, calculate their nutritional values, and fit them into your caloric allowance each day. For your convenience, two-week sample meal plans for both men and women are outlined in Chapter 15. You can initially use them as models for your own individual meal plans.

You may wonder why we haven't given you the sodium values of each food. Indeed, sodium is the enemy of any bodybuilder or health-minded individual. But the recipes in this book have been deliberately created to be low in sodium content. If you prepare the recipes strictly according to instructions, you needn't worry about your sodium intake until three to five days prior to a competition. Then, you should eat only broiled chicken and fish with no seasonings, baked potatoes, and distilled water in order to totally eliminate sodium from your diet.

Even without adding salt, you'll find the recipes in *Supercut* to be quite tasty as a result of using other, non-sodium spices. For example, you can go wild with lemon juice, dry white wine, and vinegar, all of which amazingly transform the flavors of food.

After you have prepared some of the *Supercut* recipes, we suggest that you become creative and begin to experiment with your own similar recipes. Your taste buds will guide you. A dish that may appeal to you can be less appealing to another bodybuilder and vice-versa, so it pays to individualize recipes. Just have fun with the spices when you create your own recipes.

HOW TO COOK

The first step to making cooking easy and interesting is to think ahead and make out a shopping list for about 10 of the recipes at a time. Go through the book and make a list of the ingredients of your favorite recipes, then purchase them ahead of time at a supermarket. You won't need as many ingredients as you might think, as long as you have followed the suggestions given in Tables 2-2, 2-3, and 2-4, and have stocked your cabinet and refrigerator.

Your next step is to actually prepare and cook the recipe. This involves reviewing the recipe and laying out all of the ingredients on your work surface. You should also take out the appropriate bowls, measuring cups, and other equipment needed to prepare the recipe (a comprehensive list of such equipment can be found in Table 2-1). Finally, you must know which of seven methods of cooking you will use.

Table 2-1: Basic Kitchen Equipment

Baking dish (nonstick)
Blender
Broiler (or an oven with a broiler device)
Bowls (small, medium, and large)
Containers (plastic, for storing food leftovers)
Cup (for measuring)
Frying pan (nonstick)
Grater (for grating cheese, onions, potatoes, etc.)
Knives (several, for cutting, dicing, mincing, etc.)
Mallet (for pounding meat)
Mixer (electric)
Peeler (for peeling potatoes, etc.)
Skewers (for making shish kebab dishes)
Spoons (for measuring)
Spoon (slotted, for removing food items from water and juices)
Steamer (for steaming vegetables)
Wok (optional; for cooking various Chinese dishes)

Table 2-2:
Recommended Spices and Herbs

Bay leaves	Nutmeg
Bell peppers (dry)	Onion powder
Black pepper	Oregano
Chili powder	Paprika
Chives	Parsley
Cinnamon	Red pepper (dry crushed)
Curry powder	Rosemary
Dill weed	Sage
Garlic powder	Sweet basil
Ginger	Tarragon
Marjoram	Thyme
Mustard (dry)	White pepper

Table 2-3: Basic Unrefrigerated Food Ingredients

Bread crumbs (Italian)
Bread crumbs (whole wheat)
Flour (unbleached)
Flour (whole wheat)
Rice (converted white)
Rice (brown)
Vanilla extract

Table 2-4: Basic Refrigerated Food Ingredients

Apple juice (frozen concentrate)
Fresh garlic
Lemon juice (bottled)
Lemons
Orange juice (frozen concentrate)
Parmesan cheese
Romano cheese

Table 2-5: Cooking Terms

Bake—cook in an oven or broiler with the heat surrounding the food.
Beat—mix vigorously with electric mixer, fork, or spoon.
Blend—mix together.
Boned—bones have been removed.
Broil—cook in an oven or broiler with the heat originating above the food.
Brown—fry in a nonstick pan until food is slightly browned.
Chilled—cooled in the refrigerator until cold.
Chop—cut into cubes by slicing lengthwise and then widthwise.
Chunks—large, uneven pieces.
Clove—a section of a fresh garlic, one of many that make up a head of garlic.
Combine—mix together in one bowl or pot or pan.
Core—remove the center seedy portion, as in an apple.
Cube—cut into cubes of ½ inch.
Cutlet—boned, skinned chicken or boned veal.
Dash—small sprinkle.
Deviled—finely chopped and then seasoned with hot pepper.
Dice—cut into small cubes of $1/16$ inch.
Drain—remove all water by placing in a colander or by using a slotted spoon.
Fillet—boned, flat piece of fish.
Flakes—is easily peeled and crumbles into flakes when scraped with a fork.
Fold—add by carefully mixing in a scooping, over-and-under motion.
Fry—to cook in a pan without the use of water and with or without oil.
Garnish—add to the beauty of, embellish, sprinkle.
Grate—reduce to small pieces by rubbing the food against the surface as on a metal food grater or using a food processor.
Grease—coat the bottom of a pan with oil by using a paper napkin dipped in the oil.
Marinate—soak overnight or for a few hours in a special liquid.

Mince—chop finely, almost to a liquid state.

Mix—stir briefly.

Pinch—small amount of spice placed between the thumb and forefinger and added to the food mixture.

Pulp—the pulp of a fruit. The pulp of a tomato is the seedy part.

Puree—food that has been ground or blended to a smooth saucelike or pasty consistency.

Refrigerate—place in the refrigerator to cool or keep fresh.

Saute—cook until tender in a small amount of oil or butter.

Scald—heat a liquid (such as milk) to the boiling point briefly.

Simmer—cook over a very low flame.

Skewer—place food items on a long, sharp, metal pin or thin rod.

Skim—remove from the top, (skim the fat from the top of cooled chicken soup, for example).

Skinned—skin removed before seasoning or cooking.

Slivered—cut into small pieces, long and thin.

Snipped—cut into small pieces with knife or scissors.

Sprinkle—scatter unevenly all over a food item, usually from a shaker with small openings.

Steam—cook in a vegetable steamer or double boiler so that the water never touches the food item, and the food item is cooked by the heat from the steam produced by the boiling water.

Thaw—allow to unfreeze by removing food item from the freezer.

Toss—gently mix using a large spoon or fork.

Stir-fry—fry while constantly stirring in an oil-coated pan.

Undiluted—not made weaker by the addition of water; left concentrated.

Wedge—a small section of a circular food item such as ⅛ of a tomato or a piece of pie or quiche.

The first cooking method is boiling, for which you need only a pot and water. The second method is steaming, for which you need only a pot, a vegetable steamer, and water. The third method is frying, for which you need only a nonstick frying pan. These three methods are over the heat, wherein the heat originates beneath the food.

The fourth cooking method is broiling. To broil foods, you will need a broiler or oven. Here, the heat originates above the food.

The fifth cooking method is baking, for which you need an oven or a broiler (some broilers have an oven control). In baking, heat surrounds the food being cooked.

Sixth is the charcoal broiling method, for which you will

need either a simple charcoal grill and coals, or an elabo-
rate electric charcoal and gas grill. In charcoal grilling, the
heat originates below the food being cooked, and there is
a distinct flavor imparted to the meat, a flavor appealing to
most people.

Seventh, you can use the new microwave cooking
method. We haven't suggested that you use microwave
ovens for our recipes, but you can do so without a problem
if you wish to. All you need to do is follow the conversion
table provided with the microwave unit, and you will
reduce cooking time to almost nothing.

After you have cooked the food, you only need serve it,
an action that can be tailored to your personality. You can
simply throw the food onto a paper plate or you may want
to serve it on fine china. However, it's essential that you
pay attention to the number of servings given near the bottom
of each recipe. Without doing so, you won't be able to
accurately calculate your caloric intake.

Some of the recipes are for one serving, some for two,
and others for four. You may decide to cut a recipe in half
if it serves four and make only two servings. Or, you can
double a recipe that serves only one, knowing that you can
easily eat a double portion because the recipe's caloric
content is very low.

We recommend that you don't make only one serving of
a recipe. Why not make four servings and keep some in the
refrigerator for a quickly prepared snack or a full meal
later? After all, most bodybuilders are chronically short of
time, and you'll be quite hungry when you get home from
the gym. It's nice to have a nutritious, quickly prepared
meal waiting for you, something that merely needs to be
reheated. And once you prepare a recipe and discover how
delicious it is, you'll probably want to have another
helping.

This book was created for you. You won't have to leave
the gym mumbling about having to face the same old dry
piece of fish or chicken any longer. You'll be able to enjoy
eating good foods again.

IMPORTANT REMINDERS

1. Always preheat your oven for 10–15 minutes.
2. Always preheat your broiler for 3–5 minutes.
3. Never place uncovered foods or liquids in the refrigerator. Use plastic storage containers, aluminum foil, plastic food wrap, or baggies to package leftovers.
4. When preparing a recipe, consider cooking a double amount for convenient future use.
5. Pay strict attention to the number of servings noted for each recipe.
6. Stock your cabinet and refrigerator with basic items.
7. Purchase the necessary food preparation equipment and have it on hand for all future cooking.
8. Plan your recipes for the week and prepare a shopping list of foods needed to complete these recipes.
9. Experiment with spices, lemon juice, vinegar, and white wine in your recipes. Create your own special recipes.
10. Check the sodium content only if you are five days away from your competition. Our recipes contain very few grams of sodium.

Dr. Joyce L. Vedral.

3

WEIGHT LOSS WITHOUT LOSING MUSCLE

Whether you are a bodybuilder, an athlete in another sport, or simply a health- and fitness-minded man or woman, you have probably at one time or another wanted to reduce your body fat stores. Two main types of diets are used to reduce fat stores: a low-carbohydrate regimen and a low-calorie diet. And while we will discuss both types of diets in this chapter, scientific fact strongly supports the efficacy of low-calorie dieting.

LOW-CARBOHYDRATE DIETING

The trouble with low-carbohydrate diets is that they don't work well, they are unhealthy, and they result in low energy levels and irritability. Still, there are many body-builders who have successfully followed low-carb diets. The most notable of these is Frank Zane, three-time Mr. Olympia winner. When Zane has followed a low-calorie diet, he has lost muscle mass and flattened out. But when he consumes plenty of fats in red meat and limits carbohydrate consumption, he has maximum muscle mass with good muscularity.

It will be necessary for you to experiment with both low-carbohydrate and low-calorie diets to determine which works best for you. If you are an ectomorphic type of bodybuilder who experiences a great deal of difficulty in gaining weight—as is the case with Frank Zane—you might well find that a low-carb diet works best for you when cutting up for a competition.

During the 1950s and early 1960s, low-calorie diets were the accepted way to reduce fatty tissues throughout the body. But with the advent of low-carbohydrate diets, the low-cal diet fell by the wayside. Soon everyone who wanted to lower body fat was counting carbs and *apparently* losing plenty of weight.

The low-carb diet fad was started by such books as *Dr. Atkin's Diet Revolution* and *Doctor's Quick Weight Loss Diet.* And once the ball was in motion, its own momentum kept it rolling. With numerous physicians writing popular books about the low-carbohydrate diet, it became the most widely accepted way to lose weight. The average person holds physicians in a position of trust, so it's little wonder that such a diet became so widely popular.

Additionally, a dramatic initial weight loss—as much as 6–10 pounds during the first week—provided considerable incentive for most people to maintain their low-carb diets for several weeks or months. Weight comes off very slowly with a low-carb diet, however, once you get past the initial weight loss. Biochemically, the body loses actual fat only when you take in fewer calories than your body burns up, and the low-carb diet is so high in fats that it's high in calories as well.

As a caloric source, fats are more than twice as concentrated as both proteins and carbohydrates. When metabolized, one gram of fat yields approximately nine calories, while a gram of either protein or carbohydrate yields approximately four. Therefore, when a person eats high-fat foods like beef, eggs, bacon, ham, and butter on a low-carb diet, the diet is usually too high in calories to allow body fat to be metabolized for energy.

So why the initial weight loss on a low-carb diet? It's simply because the body flushes out water that had been held by carbohydrates in the blood and muscle tissue. Each gram of carbohydrate in the human body will hold four grams of water, so when carbs are severely restricted, the body can't store water.

An inability to store water results in a very quick and

dramatic weight loss, usually occurring two to three days after the diet is initiated. At that point, the body's carbohydrate stores are depleted and water is flushed from the system.

Unfortunately, a low-carb diet also results in low energy levels because of resulting low body carbohydrate (blood sugar) levels. As the body struggles to normalize its blood sugar levels, it does burn small quantities of body fat, but that's a slow process at best. And often the body burns protein, or muscle tissue, at the same time as it metabolizes fat. This causes the loss of vital muscle tissue that most bodybuilders notice—to their horror—on low-carb diets.

Due to depressed blood sugar levels during a low-carb diet, athletes and bodybuilders also experience critically low energy levels. Anyone who has tried to train with any degree of intensity while on a low-carb diet knows how difficult it is to summon up energy after the first 15–20 minutes of a workout. Once the small amount of blood sugar your body has eked out of its fat stores has been exhausted, a workout becomes an ordeal.

Most low-carb dieters also experience marked irritability after the first few days of dieting. This is caused by the extremely high phosphorus content and low calcium content of animal proteins (other than milk products). The human body has a calcium-phosphorus balance, and when you consume too much phosphorus in relation to calcium, you get the "phosphorus jitters," becoming nervous and irritable.

In an effort to eliminate phosphorus jitters, many bodybuilders supplement their diets with chelated calcium tablets. This technique works to some extent but is usually not totally effective.

Another problem with low-carb diets is that they lead to carbohydrate binge eating. **Richard Baldwin** (two-time American Middleweight Champion) notes, "I follow a low-carbohydrate diet prior to a competition and constantly must guard against falling off of the diet. I seem to crave carbohydrates after the first couple of weeks on the diet, and it's a chore to avoid them. But if I fall off the wagon and eat some high-carb junk food, I'm finished; I'll find it almost impossible to get back on a strict diet until my carbo binge has run its course."

Our final objection to the low-carb diet is that, nutritionally, it's poorly balanced. By eliminating many fruits and vegetables from your diet, you deprive your body of numerous vitamins, minerals, and enzymes it needs to maintain optimum health. Granted, most of these nutrients can be replaced by taking food supplements, but this practice is akin to stripping wheat grain of all its nutrients by milling it into white flour and then replacing the lost nutrients with synthetic vitamins.

It's relatively easy to follow a low-carbohydrate diet. You'll first need to purchase an inexpensive carbohydrate gram counter at a drugstore. With this booklet in hand, you can determine how many grams of carbohydrate are contained in each serving of the foods you consume.

Initiate your low-carb diet by restricting carbohydrate intake each day to 150 grams for one week. This will essentially amount to little more than cutting from your diet junk foods high in sugar and flour. Then, each succeeding week, you should progressively drop 20–30 grams of carbohydrate from your diet until you're down to a minimum intake of 30–50 grams per day. Ingesting fewer than 30 grams of carbohydrate per day is very unhealthy and destructive to your body.

You will eat plenty of fat while on a low-carb regimen, so beef, cheese, and even butter are permitted. Looking at your carbohydrate counter booklet, however, you will find that you must avoid tasty, nutritious foods such as fruit, some vegetables, grains, seeds, nuts, and any sort of sweet foods.

Following is a meal plan for one day of relatively strict low-carbohydrate dieting.

- *Breakfast*—steak, eggs, coffee with artificial sweetener, supplements.
- *Lunch*—broiled chicken, green vegetable, iced tea with artificial sweetener, supplements.
- *Preworkout Snack*—half a cantaloupe.

- *Dinner*—roast beef, green salad with oil and vinegar dressing, hard cheese, coffee or tea with artificial sweetener, supplements.
- *Snack*—hard-boiled eggs, cold cuts.

You'll need to be a little careful with your selection of food supplements when following a low-carb diet since some of them contain carbohydrate. Most notably, desiccated liver tablets—used by many bodybuilders to increase training energy—are roughly 30 percent carbohydrate. If you consume desiccated liver when adhering to a low-carbohydrate diet, the carbos in the liver must also be counted.

LOW-FAT/LOW-CALORIE DIETING

So how *do* you diet effectively, have plenty of energy for workouts, avoid the phosphorus jitters, and still remain healthy? Simply put, you go on a low-fat/low-calorie diet! And that's what the recipes in Chapters 7–13 are all about—taste-pleasing, low-calorie dieting.

Fats are twice as concentrated a source of potential energy as protein or carbohydrates. So it makes good sense to cut back drastically on fats and to eat primarily protein and carbohydrates when reducing calories before a competition or whenever you want to lose fat.

The body needs only 10–20 grams of fat per day for optimum nerve and skin health, and even low-fat protein foods like fish and chicken breasts contain some fat. Therefore, you needn't worry about taking in too little fat, only too much!

A low-fat/low-calorie diet is quite well balanced and healthy for the body because most fresh fruits and vegetables are fairly low in calories. And, as you know, your body needs substantial amounts of fruit and vegetables to provide natural vitamins, minerals, and enzymes.

As a health bonus, low-fat eating is very good for heart and vascular health. Many researchers cite animal fats as contributing to heart attacks, strokes, and hardening of the arteries. By eliminating animal fats from your diet—or by restricting them to small daily amounts—you reduce the risk of heart and vascular disease at the same time as you reduce body fat levels.

Workout energy is not a problem on a low-fat diet, because your body's preferred source of workout energy is carbohydrate from fresh fruits and vegetables. Such natural sugars are quickly and easily metabolized for workout energy. Fats, on the other hand, are used for long-term energy needs because they are metabolized more slowly than carbohydrates.

In fine-tuning your carbohydrate intake, you should note that simple carbohydrates, such as those found in fruit and refined foods, are quickly digested and suffused into the bloodstream. Complex carbohydrates, such as those found in vegetables, grains, seeds, and nuts, on the other hand, are more slowly digested and released into the bloodstream. So consume fruit for quick energy and vegetables for more sustained energy flow.

Phosphorus jitters are also no problem on a low-fat/low-calorie diet. That's because fish and chicken are lower in phosphorus than beef and pork, and you can drink milk on a low-fat diet. As long as you include the milk calories in your daily calorie count, you can easily drink one or two glasses of nonfat milk each day. You can also eat low-fat cheeses, cottage cheese, and yogurt. All milk products are high in calcium, so phosphorus jitters are eliminated on low-fat diets.

Above all, low-fat dieting is without equal for knocking fat off the human body. After many years of low-carb dieting, **Dennis Tinerino** (Pro Mr. Universe) switched to low-fat/low-calorie dieting and noted, "I'm surprised how good this low-fat diet has been for me. I've been able to build more mass than in any previous year, while retaining my usual low body fat levels. And the white meats included in a low-fat diet are much easier to digest than the beef I ate when following a low-carbohydrate diet."

A low-fat diet is easy to follow. Simply drop beef and pork from your diet, replacing them with broiled fish or chicken breasts (without the skin, which contains quite a lot of fat), and you'll considerably reduce the overall caloric content of your diet.

Other high-fat foods that should be eliminated or reduced include butter; cooking and salad oils; all nuts and peanut butter; cream, full-fat milk, and full-fat milk products; corn; bananas; avocados; baked goods with shortening; sunflower and other types of seeds; some grains (such as wheat); and many artificial creamers. All of these foods can be replaced with fresh fruits and vegetables low in fat.

The next dietetic refinement you can make is to eat lower-calorie fruits and vegetables. Low-cal produce includes grapefruit, strawberries, cantaloupe, honeydew melons, peaches, lemons, pineapples, cucumbers, mushrooms, lettuce, spinach, celery, seed sprouts, tomatoes, green peppers, squash, cherries, and potatoes (baked, no butter or sour cream). These fruits and vegetables can be eaten in place of such higher-calorie produce as bananas, oranges, apricots, apples, watermelon, pears, yams, sweet potatoes, and grapes.

Keep a Record

Many competing bodybuilders find they need to keep a record of what they eat, totaling up their calories each day. To stay under a certain caloric level every day when you're eating a varied diet, it's very helpful to keep a food diary.

Buy a blank notebook and a good calorie counter booklet, then simply record the calories for everything you eat and drink. Women can begin a diet by eating about 1,800 calories per day; men can start with 3,000. Then, if you need to lose weight more quickly, reduce the caloric intake progressively (200–300 calories per week). Don't rush the diet, however, because fat will come off gradually even on a very harsh diet.

This is where the recipes and meal plans included in this book pay off most handsomely. Simply choose individual recipes and meal plans that place you within the caloric parameters of your diet at each particular stage and stick to the diet. For each 3,500 calories you burn off or don't eat in the first place, you will lose one pound of useless body fat!

Following is an example of a relatively strict low-fat precontest diet.

- *Breakfast*—bran cereal with nonfat milk, egg whites, half a cantaloupe, coffee or tea.
- *Snack*—one piece of fruit.
- *Lunch*—broiled fish, steamed rice, green vegetable, iced tea with lemon.
- *Snack*—one piece of fruit.
- *Dinner*—broiled chicken breast (skinned before cooking), dry baked potato, coffee or iced tea.

Many other sample daily meal plans are presented in Chapters 14 and 15. Chapter 14 presents sample daily meal plans for one-week periods for both men and women, with the caloric consumption for each day calculated precisely. And Chapter 15 presents a variety of meal plans used by the top bodybuilders.

As you become more experienced with low-fat eating, you'll be able to tell instinctively when you've cut your calories enough. And you'll be able to play with endless combinations of foods each day. You'll even be able to eat a little red meat now and then, as long as you count the extra calories it contains and balance them with a fish meal.

Low-Fat Dieting Hints

1. Use plain vinegar and/or lemon juice for salad dressing rather than oil and vinegar or other oil-containing dressings. Use vinegar as much as possible since it helps to burn fat.
2. Buy whole-grain bread in a health food store, being sure it's baked without oil, butter, or shortening. Such relatively unrefined grain products are quite low in calories when compared to regular grocery store bread.
3. If you can make a choice between fish and chicken for a meal, choose fish since it's significantly lower in calories.
4. Eat bread plain, without butter, jam, jelly, or peanut butter. It isn't the bread that's so fattening but the

stuff put on it. Similarly, eat baked potatoes without the butter or sour cream.

5. If you have a craving for sugar or junk food—which you should avoid—eat a serving of a naturally sweet fruit like strawberries or a melon.

6. Avoid excess sodium, such as in salt, dietetic foods, and artificially sweetened drinks. Sodium retains excess water in the body. Instead of a diet soda, drink iced tea with lemon.

7. If you must drink milk or eat milk products, use only those made from nonfat milk.

8. Fry nothing. Broil, boil, or bake fish and chicken. Try broiling fish or chicken over a charcoal fire for added flavor. Before cooking poultry, remove the skin, which contains large amounts of fat.

9. Steam vegetables instead of boiling them. Boiling leaches out many vitamins and minerals. Do *not* add butter or margarine to the steamed vegetables.

10. Cook with herbs and spices as much as possible. By using different kinds, you can easily make chicken breasts taste different every day of the week.

Conclusion

When following a tight low-fat/low-calorie diet, you will notice obvious changes in your physique virtually every day. However, you will probably notice a small diminishment in the amount of weight you are able to use in each exercise under nondiet circumstances. This loss in exercise poundages is primarily due to mild residual fatigue present when dieting strictly. Generally speaking, you will always feel a bit fatigued and low in energy when correctly maintaining a caloric deficit. Champion bodybuilders consider this fatigue and lack of energy as merely part of the territory when following a low-calorie diet prior to a competition.

Low-fat/low-calorie dieting is definitely the answer to problems bodybuilders, other athletes, and fitness-minded individuals have experienced in losing fat. Give it a try, and you'll find that the low-fat diet is truly miraculous!

SODIUM CONTROL

As just mentioned, sodium has a tremendous affinity for water, and excess sodium in your diet can hold water in your system, blurring out your hard-earned muscular definition. Therefore, the recipes presented in this book are purposely low in sodium content.

Still, you must exercise care in controlling sodium in your diet. Primarily, you must *never* add table salt to any of your food. And, you should avoid those artificial sweeteners and artificially sweetened beverages containing sodium saccharide as a sweetening agent.

THE CYTOTOXIC DIET

Bodybuilders with chronic water retention problems should experiment with the cytotoxic diet, which shows great promise for the elimination of excess water. The theory behind this diet is that minor allergies to various foods cause water retention and a host of other health problems, and elimination of these foods from the diet reverses the problems they cause.

Cytotoxic is a hybrid word, *cyto* meaning "cell" and *toxic* meaning "killing." One of the leading exponents of the testing and dietary procedures related to the cytotoxic diet is Dr. James Braly, a physician practicing in Encino, California. Dr. Braly runs the Optimum Health Labs in Suite 202 of the West Valley Medical Center, 5353 Balboa Boulevard, Encino, California, and he was interviewed about the cytotoxic diet.

Dr. Braly defines himself as an ecological physician. "There are two types of physicians," he explained. "The traditional doctor will treat the *symptoms* of diseases, while ecological doctors will look for and treat the *root causes* of diseases. And in many cases, diseases are caused by chemical food allergies."

Dr. Braly provided the following list of common food allergy symptoms:

Physical Symptoms

Head: Headaches, faintness, dizziness, feeling of fullness in the head, excessive drowsiness or sleepiness soon after eating, insomnia.

Eyes, ears, nose and throat: Runny nose, stuffy nose, excessive mucus formation, watery eyes, blurring of vision, ringing of the ears, earache, fullness in the ears, fluid in the middle ear, hearing loss, recurrent ear infections, itching ear, ear drainage, sore throats, chronic cough, gagging, canker sores, itching of the roof of the mouth, recurrent sinusitis.

Heart and lungs: Palpitations, increased heart rate, rapid heart rate (tachycardia), asthma, congestion in the chest, hoarseness.

Gastrointestinal: Nausea, vomiting, diarrhea, constipation, bloating after meals, belching, colitis, flatulence (passing gas), feeling of fullness in the stomach long after finishing a meal, abdominal pains or cramps.

Skin: Hives, rashes, eczema, dermatitis, pallor.

Other Symptoms: Chronic fatigue; weakness; muscle aches and pains; joint aches and pains; swelling of the hands, feet, or ankles; urinary tract symptoms (frequency, urgency); vaginal itching; vaginal discharge; hunger (and its close ally, "binge or spree" eating).

Psychological Symptoms

Anxiety, "panic attacks," depression, "crying jags," aggressive behavior, irritability, mental dullness, mental lethargy, confusion, excessive daydreaming, hyperactivity, restlessness, learning disabilities, poor work habits, slurred speech, stuttering, inability to concentrate, indifference.

The cytotoxic test is foolproof. A blood sample is taken and centrifuged to remove the plasma and white blood cells, and then small drops of white blood cells are placed on microscope slides with tiny concentrated samples of nearly 150 elemental foods. After two hours, the slides are examined under a microscope. If the body is not allergic to a food, the white blood cells will remain normal. But if there is an allergic reaction, the blood cells will become structurally changed, or—in the case of a severe food allergy—the cell walls will rupture.

"By simply avoiding the foods you are allergic to, you can alleviate most of these symptoms," **Dr. Braly** told us. "We also recommend that you eat the nonoffending foods rotationally, repeating a particular food in your diet no more often than every four days. This helps to prevent food allergies, which often develop from simply eating a food too frequently. It also induces you to eat a wider variety of foods. The average American eats only about 15 different foods over and over again. Eating two to three times that number will automatically give you a healthier diet.

"You will most likely notice that you are allergic to most of the foods you eat frequently. That's because allergenic foods cause an actual addiction, and your body begins to crave those foods. So if you're allergic to sucrose, you'll feel temporarily better when you're eating a lot of sugar-laden foods.

"To illustrate how a food addiction works, let's examine how smoking tobacco becomes an addiction, because the cases are identical. No one who ever began smoking cigarettes liked the taste of tobacco or the body's reaction to the first few cigarettes. But the nicotine in tobacco is a powerful poison, and the body's defense systems are forced to go into high gear to fight off the toxins. Thus, for a few minutes after smoking a cigarette, a smoker feels a physical and mental boost.

"The same thing happens when you eat an allergenic food. The food is toxic to your body, and it causes the body's defense mechanisms to swing into action. You feel a definite boost. But, unfortunately, these toxins have long-range harmful effects on the body.

"Food allergies are most often manifested in the body as inflammations, which is why arthritis is a common by-product of food allergies. And since inflammations hold a great deal of water in the body, a bodybuilder could look bloated onstage, even if he had the bare minimum of body fat.

"Keep in mind here that we are not talking about acute allergic reactions to foods, such as a person breaking out in hives a few minutes after eating strawberries. We're talking about insidious, low-intensity food allergies, the symptoms of which are often confused with other types of diseases.

"The reason, therefore, that we eat some foods all the time," Dr. Braly continued, "is that they give you a lift. You feel good when you eat them, or at least you feel good for a short time after eating a certain food. So, subconsciously, you begin to crave that food because it's the one that makes you feel better. And often such foods will also alleviate the allergy symptoms temporarily."

We would like to give you a sample meal plan for cytotoxic eating, as we did for both low-carbohydrate and low-fat dieting. However, everyone has different food allergies, which would make a sample diet irrelevant to 99 percent of the bodybuilding population. If you decide to follow a cytotoxic diet, your actual meal plans will be worked out with the assistance of your physician *after* you have identified your own unique allergens.

Dr. Braly then told us, "Within a few weeks of eliminating the allergenic foods from your diet, you'll notice some drastic changes in your physical and psychological well-being. One immediate result is a marked weight loss. Some patients lose up to 10–15 pounds in two or three weeks. This is primarily water that's flushed from the system once the allergy-induced inflammations have abated.

"The key to following the cytotoxic diet successfully is eating simply. Since you don't know for sure what is in most restaurant dishes, you'll have to eat mostly at home, and primarily you'll need to eat basic, simple meals. Something like Beef Stroganoff or Macaroni and Cheese will be virtually impossible to eat because of the wide range of ingredients in each of these dishes."

Dr. Braly offered a bit of concluding advice to all

bodybuilders and fitness-minded individuals: "Most people are allergic to milk products and/or grains. Even if you can't take the cytotoxic test, it would be a good idea to drop these two food groups from your diet. [Fresh green vegetables provide calcium and rice provides fiber in replacing milk and grains. Further discussion of milk can be found in the next chapter.] If you do, you probably will notice a considerable improvement in your physical and mental health in only two or three weeks!"

4
MUSCULAR WEIGHT GAIN

Throughout the history of bodybuilding, men and women have tried every possible method to add muscular body weight to their physiques. They tried exotic dietary regimens and even more exotic bodybuilding training programs to accomplish this goal, often to little avail. With the advanced state of dietary and training technology available today, however, it's relatively easy to gain muscular body weight at an acceptable rate of speed. And, we'll thoroughly discuss all of these weight-gaining procedures in this chapter.

From the late 1930s through the mid-1970s, the classic method of gaining muscular body weight—a method used by luminaries such as Bill Pearl (four-time Mr. Universe), Scott Wilson (IFBB Mr. International), and many others— was to bulk up 20 or more pounds through heavy training and even heavier eating during an off-season cycle. After reaching a high body weight, a man would then train lighter and diet strictly during a peaking phase to display greater mass at contest time. Bulking up and training down worked for many bodybuilders, but the method had enough drawbacks to lead ultimately to its retirement by serious competitive bodybuilders.

The most extreme example of a man successfully bulking up and then training down was Bruce Randall, who won the NABBA Mr. Universe title during the late 1950s. At a height slightly over 6'1", he began his bulking program weighing only 180 pounds, his goal merely to gain enough weight to make his military base's football team. But within a few short weeks, Bruce was over the 220 mark and hooked on the iron.

Following a program of very heavy eating and training with gargantuan poundages, Randall soon reached a body weight of 401 pounds. Granted, he appeared corpulent, but there was plenty of muscle under the fat. Just for openers, he could do a Good Morning exercise with a barbell weighing nearly twice his body weight, and he could Standing Press more than 400 pounds at a time when only two or three world-class weightlifters could duplicate the feat.

Eventually, Randall's goals changed, and he became determined to reduce his weight until he reached competitive bodybuilding condition. He gradually cut back on his food portions, trained much lighter, and did aerobic workouts. In less than 20 weeks he lost 200 pounds of fat and looked sensationally cut up. There wasn't a millimeter of loose skin anywhere on his body, despite the rapid gain and loss of such a massive amount of weight. Within a couple of years he had built up to a diamond-hard 225 and won his Mr. Universe title.

Other modern bodybuilders have had less luck with bulking up and training down. Listen to **Lou Ferrigno** (Mr. America, Mr. International, twice IFBB Mr. Universe, and a noted film star): "Early in my competitive career when I weighed 220 pounds in hard shape, I decided to bulk up and then train down over a one-year period of time. I trained as heavily as possible, mainly on basic exercises, and ate virtually everything that wasn't nailed down. Seven months later I scaled a huge, soft 305 pounds at 6'5" in height.

"With five months to go until my competition, I began training down, confident that I'd put on 15–20 pounds of solid muscle mass by bulking up. I did everything right for my contest—the low-calorie diet, aerobics, high-intensity bodybuilding workouts—and reached sharp contest shape again. But what do you think I weighed after the ordeal of losing all that fat? Only 222, two measly pounds more than

I'd scaled a year before. I could only conclude after this experiment that the old bulking-up-and-training-down procedure was worthless for me. And in the intervening years I've discovered that very few bodybuilders make good gains following this outmoded program. I'd advise against using it.

"As far as I'm concerned, it's best to stay within 6–8 pounds of hard competitive condition and slowly gain muscle mass throughout the year. Using this philosophy, I've put on as much as 10–12 pounds of awesomely dense muscle tissue in a year, which made a tremendous difference in my appearance!"

Robby Robinson (Mr. America, Mr. World, Mr. Universe, and a Pro Grand Prix Champion) agrees with Ferrigno: "The days of bulking up and then training down are over. Sure, it makes you feel bigger when you put on 10 or 20 pounds, but it's fat, not muscle. You end up feeling skinny and light when you get rid of that covering of fat, but what you have left is the real you. Psychologically, after years of trying to get bigger and bigger, this is tough to take.

"One of the biggest mistakes bodybuilders make is eating too much. Then they have to work extrahard in the gym to burn off those extra calories. I believe that it's better to restrict your caloric intake in the first place, rather than having to waste energy burning up fat later. When you're burning fat, you're not building much muscle. So why bother?"

Women bodybuilders echo the feelings of Robinson and Ferrigno. Says **Rachel McLish** (World Pro Champion, twice Miss Olympia), "No one, man or woman, will build muscle very quickly unless the bodybuilder is foolish enough to resort to anabolic drug use. I always advise patience. Pay your dues in the gym with heavy, high-intensity workouts; follow a balanced, high-protein diet; and you'll slowly, steadily, and inevitably make good gains in muscle mass. There's no other way around it!"

NOT BY BREAD ALONE

This chapter is primarily about diet for weight gain, but we would be remiss if we failed to discuss the role of heavy exercise in the weight-gaining process and give you a proven muscle-mass augmentation workout schedule.

One of the most important maxims in bodybuilding training is: the more weight you can use for a certain number of reps in an exercise, the larger will be the muscles that move the weight. In other words, the stronger you are, the more massive you will be. But keep in mind that this is a relative concept. There are a lot of very massive individuals who can't Squat or Bench the weights that a tiny powerlifter can hoist. So, your object should be to increase your own power gradually but steadily, with a variety of basic bodybuilding exercises for all parts of your body.

How Often?

You should train less frequently during a weight-gaining cycle than when trying to cut up for a competition. In order to build muscle mass at the fastest possible speed, you will need plenty of time to recuperate fully between workouts. Training six times per week simply doesn't allow you sufficient recuperation time. Therefore, we suggest that you train four days per week, hitting half of your body on Mondays and Thursdays and the other half on Tuesdays and Fridays.

Alternately, you can follow the newly popular four-day training cycle, working out for three straight days and then resting one day prior to starting up a new workout cycle. As long as you have no objection to working out on weekends from time to time, this four-day cycle will work fine during a mass-building training phase.

You will find examples of four-day split routines in Figure 5–1 on page 31 and an example of a four-day training cycle in Figure–2, also on page 31.

How Much?

I (Bill Reynolds) have been involved in bodybuilding for more than 25 years and have interviewed literally every champion bodybuilder you've read about in various muscle magazines over the past 10 years. With this amount of

---

Figure 5-1: Four-Day Split Routines.

ALTERNATIVE ONE

Monday/Thursday	Tuesday/Friday
Abdominals	Abdominals
Chest	Thighs
Upper Back	Upper Arms
Deltoids	Forearms
Calves	Calves

ALTERNATIVE TWO

Monday/Thursday	Tuesday/Friday
Abdominals	Abdominals
Chest	Back
Shoulders	Thighs
Upper Arms	Forearms
Calves	Calves

Figure 5-2: Four-Day Training Cycle.

Day One	Day Two	Day Three	Day Four
Abdominals	Abdominals	Abdominals	Rest
Chest	Thighs	Shoulders	
Back	Forearms	Upper Arms	
Calves	Calves	Forearms	

experience behind me, I have concluded that novice, intermediate, and even advanced bodybuilders who aren't making good gains invariably are losing out because they are overtraining. They are simply doing too much work for their bodies to be able to recover between workouts and grow in mass and strength.

Individual bodybuilders—whether they be men or women—have varying recovery rates between workouts. Some can do 20 sets per muscle group and still recover enough between sessions to make great gains. Others can probably do no more than five or six sets for most muscle groups without stepping over the fine line that exists between training with optimum intensity and training too much.

Unless you are a superexperienced, contest-level body-builder, I firmly believe that you will make your best gains during a mass-building cycle if you restrict your training of large muscle groups (e.g., thighs, back, chest, and deltoids) to 8–12 total sets per workout. And for other body parts, you should do 6–8 total sets. Generally speaking, larger and more complex muscle groups need a few more sets of work than the smaller and less complex body parts.

These parameters for total sets per body part do not include two or three light warm-up sets for each muscle group. And with a bit of time and astute use of your instinctive training ability, you may discover that you actually need to do a few less or a few more sets than what I recommend. However, these outlined parameters for sets are a good starting point, and they will work for at least 90 percent of all aspiring bodybuilders.

Basic Exercises

You should concentrate your efforts during a heavy training cycle primarily on basic exercises that work the largest muscle groups of your body, usually in concert with smaller body parts. A good example of a basic exercise for your chest is the Bench Press, which works not only your pectorals but also your anterior deltoids and triceps.

The opposite of a basic exercise is an isolation movement, which is best used during a peaking cycle when you're trying to define and add details to your physique. An isolation exercise works a specific muscle group by itself with minimum involvement of other muscles in your body. A good example of an isolation movement for your pectorals would be Pec Deck Flyes.

In Figure 5–3 on page 33, you will find typical basic and isolation exercises for each muscle group in your body.

Figure 5-3: Basic and Isolation Exercises.

BODY PART	BASIC EXERCISES	ISOLATION EXERCISES
Thighs	Squats, Front Squats, Leg Presses, Stiff-Legged Deadlifts	Leg Extensions, Leg Curls, Cable Adductions, Cable Abductions
Back	Upright Rows, Barbell/ Dumbbell Bent Rows, Seated Pulley Rows, Deadlifts, Chins, Lat Pulldowns	Nautilus Pullovers, Bent-Arm Pullovers, Cross-Bench Pullovers, Shrugs, Hyperextensions
Chest	Incline/Flat/Decline Bench Presses, Dips	Dumbbell/Cable Flyes (all angles), Pec Deck Flyes, Cable Crossovers
Shoulders	Barbell/Dumbbell/ Machine Presses, Upright Rows	Front/Side/Bent Laterals, Cable Laterals
Biceps	Barbell Curls, Preacher Curls, Chins	Concentration Curls, Machine Curls
Triceps	Close-Grip Bench Presses, Dips	Barbell/Dumbbell Triceps Extensions, Pulley Pushdowns
Forearms	Barbell/Pulley Reverse Curls	Barbell/Dumbbell Wrist Curls
Calves	Jump Squats	Standing/Seated Calf Raises
Abdominals	Sit-Ups, Leg Raises	Crunches, Side Bends

The Pyramid System

The easiest way to lift heavy weights consistently in your exercises, and to warm up sufficiently to avoid progress-stalling injuries, is to use the pyramid system of training with each exercise. In a true pyramid, you will work up in weight and down in reps with each succeeding set until you reach a peak weight, then work back down in weight and up in reps until you reach your original starting point.

Figure 5-4: Sample Pyramid Training Scheme.

SET NUMBER	POUNDAGE	REPS
1	135	12
2	225	10
3	275	8
4	315	6
5	355	4
6	375	2
7	255	maximum

For our purposes, however, we will use a half-pyramid in which we just work up in weight and down in reps each set to a peak, then perhaps do one high-rep pump set with a light weight after reaching the peak poundage.

In Figure 5–4 above, you will find a sample pyramid scheme for the Squat exercise (weights have been chosen arbitrarily).

We think your best bet during a heavy training cycle is to pyramid at least one basic exercise per body part, then perhaps add another movement with either straight sets or a modified pyramid in which you do just the 10-8-6-4 series of reps. For example, your chest training program might look like this:

Exercise	Sets	Reps
Bench Presses	7	12-10-8-6-4-2-max
Barbell Incline Presses	4	10-8-6-4

We've known bodybuilders who have made tremendous gains in both mass and strength while following a pyramid system of reps and weights similar to what we have just outlined. Tom Platz, for example, put more than 100 pounds on his Squat in just three months using this system, and that was the beginning of his unbelievable thigh mass and muscularity. You might not make gains quite that quickly, but you'll certainly gain like a madman/woman if you follow this pyramid power system.

You will find a suggested weight-gaining training program in Figure 5–5 on page 35.

Figure 5-5: Suggested Weight-Gain Training Program.

MONDAY/THURSDAY

Exercise	Sets	Reps
Incline Sit-Ups	3-4	15-25
Leg Presses (45-degree machine)	7	12-10-8-6-4-2-max
Leg Curls	5	10-8-6-4-max
Deadlifts (once a week)	4	10-8-6-4-max
Seated Pulley Rows	6	12-10-8-6-4-max
Rotating Dumbbell Shrugs	4	10-8-6-5
Barbell Curls	5	10-8-6-4-max
Barbell Wrist Curls	4	12-10-8-6
Standing Calf Raises	5	15-12-10-8-6

TUESDAY/FRIDAY

Exercise	Sets	Reps
Hanging Leg Raises	3-4	10-15
Smith Machine Incline Presses	6	10-8-6-4-2-max
Barbell Bench Presses	4	10-8-6-4
Military Presses	5	10-8-6-4-2
Upright Rows	4	10-8-6-4
Lying Barbell Triceps Extensions	5	10-8-6-4-max
Reverse Curls	4	10-8-6-4
Seated Calf Raises	7	15-12-10-8-6-4-max

Mental Approach

Virtually all of the biggest bodybuilders feel that the mind is the key to success in increasing mass and power during a heavy training cycle. Training and diet *are* important, but mental approach is the glue that holds the entire process together. Think big, and you'll eventually become big.

Visualization is the key to fostering a proper mental approach to mass- and power-building. Visualization is merely a creative form of daydreaming in which you assume a comfortable position on your back and then conjure up a realistic mental image of how you eventually want your physique to appear.

The best time to practice visualization is at night, just before you retire for the evening. When you're lying in bed, preparing to sleep, you are already relaxed, and you have minimum chance of distraction.

Project a visual image against the insides of your eyelids, just as if your mind were a movie projector and your eyelids the screen. Imagine your physique in a much more massive, muscular, and powerful form, visualizing every detail of muscular development. Also try to feel what it would be like inside that body, flexing those massive new muscles. Once you have this image clearly in focus, you'll find it quite pleasurable to hold on to it. Hold it for at least 10–15 minutes, even longer if you wish to. The more realistic the image, the longer you hold it, and the more frequently you use this visualization technique, the more quickly you will be able to attain the physique you wish to have.

THE KEY NUTRIENT: PROTEIN

Other than your bones, most of your tissues and organs and even your body's enzymes are formed from protein. A few of these bodily components made up largely from protein are your skin, hair, nails, heart, lungs, and vascular system. And crucially for bodybuilders, skeletal muscles are formed primarily from protein, the main reason that serious bodybuilders and other athletes follow high-protein diets.

The protein in human muscle and other tissues is formed from 22 smaller building blocks called *amino acids*. Fourteen of these amino acids can be formed within your body from virtually any foods you consume. The other 8 amino acids must be consumed in the food you eat, since they cannot be formed within your body; hence, they are called *essential amino acids*.

Regardless of how hard you pump iron in the gym, you won't be able to build additional muscle mass unless you consume protein that contains all eight essential amino acids. A protein food containing these essential amino acids is called a *complete protein* food, and complete protein foods come primarily from animal sources. Some of the richest protein foods, then, are milk and milk products, eggs, fish, poultry, and red meat, all of which should be included in your weight-gaining diet.

By and large, vegetarian foods provide *incomplete protein*. This means they lack one or more of the eight essential amino acids, one reason that the most successful vegetarian bodybuilders rely heavily on eggs and milk products in their diets. "Sprouted seeds are a very complete protein source," avers **Andreas Cahling** (Mr. International and today's leading vegetarian bodybuilder). Soybeans are also close to being a source of complete protein, but they still lag far behind animal-source proteins.

Biochemists have established a Protein Efficiency Ratio (PER) that evaluates how completely and easily each of a wide variety of protein foods is digested and moved into the bloodstream where it can be assimilated into muscle tissue or other bodily tissues. The PER is based on a scale with egg white at the extreme top and other foods ranked sequentially below egg white. Fish meal and milk rank a bit below egg white in PER, while poultry and red meats trail considerably in PER. Bringing up the rear in terms of PER are such vegetarian protein sources as seeds, grains, nuts, beans, and potatoes.

Your object as a bodybuilder attempting to gain muscular body weight is to consume the best-quality proteins, those animal-source protein foods with high PER ratings. But we are sure it hasn't escaped your notice that these foods are among the most expensive in a grocery store, so it will be advantageous to learn to combine foods with lower PERs with high-PER foods to bring up the PER value of the lesser-value proteins.

People in countries with poor economies have been using this food-combining process for centuries, intuitively completing the amino acid count of vegetarian foods by combining them with milk and other high-PER foods. Following are several such food combinations that will improve your consumption of high-quality protein without causing you extreme expense:

- BEANS + RICE + MILK
- CORN + CHEESE
- RICE + TOFU + FISH

As you will notice in a later section of this chapter, it will be advantageous to purchase a book such as the *Nutrition Almanac* (Revised edition, McGraw-Hill, 1979) and learn how many grams of protein are contained in each of the protein foods that you normally consume.

Milk

Most weight-gain diets are based heavily on milk and various milk products. Indeed, many bodybuilders consider milk to be a perfect food with its high concentrations of protein, fats, carbohydrates, vitamins, and minerals. Still, there are many individuals suffering from a malady called *galactose intolerance* who cannot comfortably drink milk.

Galactose intolerance results when a person loses his or her ability to produce the stomach enzyme *lactase*, which is required to digest lactose, the sugar found in milk. Stomach bloating shortly after drinking milk is the most common symptom of galactose intolerance. Other symptoms include drowsiness, lack of energy, and a general feeling of discomfort.

Galactose intolerance becomes more common as a person grows older, and it is far more common among men than among women and among races with darker skins than among light-skinned individuals. And other than making it uncomfortable for you to drink milk, galactose intolerance is not otherwise harmful.

There are two ways in which you can overcome galactose intolerance and include milk and milk products in your weight-gaining diet. The first of these is to purchase lactase tablets at a drugstore and take one or two of the tablets with each glass of milk. The lactase in these tablets merely replaces the lactase your stomach no longer produces, allowing you to naturally digest the sugar in the milk you drink.

Second, you can avoid milk itself but eat milk products such as hard cheese, cottage cheese, and yogurt, which have all had the lactose removed from the milk as it was processed. There's plenty of muscle-building protein in cheese and other processed milk products.

Supermarkets primarily sell pasteurized milk and milk products. Harmful bacteria in milk killed thousands of infants before Louis Pasteur discovered that heating milk would kill these harmful bacteria and prevent disease. Unfortunately, however, pasteurization also kills many potentially valuable bacterial agents in milk. And heating milk also denatures many of the nutrients in the food.

"Consuming certified raw milk and milk products is the answer," states **Andreas Cahling**. "Raw milk comes from cows regularly inspected by the government and certified to be free from disease. As a result, raw milk is both safe to drink and highly nutritious. I recommend it."

Raw milk and raw milk products are widely available in health food stores, as well as in many supermarkets. And they cost virtually the same amount of money as the equivalent pasteurized products. Therefore, if raw milk is available in your area, you should include it in your diet.

How Much Protein?

Depending on the size of your stomach and your relative digestive efficiency, your body can digest and make ready for assimilation into muscle tissue 20–30 grams of protein each time you eat. And these figures become important when choosing foods and how much of each food to eat at each meal. Too little protein at a meal, and you simply won't supply your muscles with sufficient amino acids to allow for growth. But if you eat too much protein, you can clog up your digestive system, preventing your body from using the food you've eaten.

As long as you are consuming first-class, complete protein foods, you should eat 20–30 grams of protein each time you sit down to a meal. If your build is relatively small, eat something close to the lower of these two figures; if you are large, eat up to 30 grams per meal; and if you are taking digestive supports (which are discussed a bit later in this chapter), you can also eat a bit more protein, perhaps 5 grams more than normal at each meal.

The Food and Drug Administration (FDA) recommends approximately ½ gram of protein per pound of body weight for basic tissue maintenance. For bodybuilders and active athletes, we feel that something between ¾ and 1 gram of protein per pound of body weight is more appropriate. Therefore, a 180-pound man should consume 135–180 grams of first-class protein per day; a 120-pound woman should eat 90–120 grams of protein each day.

But if you're good at math, you will already have calculated that a 180-pound man eating 30 grams of protein three times per day will consume only 90 grams each day, a figure well short of the 135–180 range. Surely, there *must* be a way in which a person can consume, digest, and make ready for assimilation more total protein each day. There is!

The answer to this knotty problem is to eat more than three meals per day but to keep them small and made up of adequate amounts of complete protein foods. Rather than the traditional two or three large meals each day, bodybuilders, athletes, and others interested in muscular weight gain should eat four to six times per day. And, the 180-pound man who consumes 30 grams of protein at each meal will end up consuming 180 grams of protein per day if he can eat six times.

Figure 5-6: Suggested Weight-Gain Menu.

Meal 1 (8:00 A.M.)—cheese omelette, milk, supplements.

Meal 2 (10:30 A.M.)—tuna salad, slice of hard cheese, orange juice

Meal 3 (1:00 P.M.)—broiled chicken, rice, small salad, iced tea, supplements.

Meal 4 (3:30 P.M.)—protein drink, supplements.

Meal 5 (6:00 P.M.)—broiled steak, baked potato, green vegetable, milk, supplements.

Meal 6 (8:30 P.M.)—cold cuts, yogurt, raw nuts and seeds, glass of milk.

These small, frequent meals should be evenly spaced over the day, allowing for no more than three hours between feedings. A suggested weight-gain menu is presented in Figure 5–6 above. Take a good look at it and feel free to adapt it to include the foods that you prefer to eat, just as long as you also stay within the other guidelines presented in this chapter.

Valuable Food Supplements

There are several food supplements that will help you gain muscular body weight more efficiently, and we discuss them briefly in this section. For more detailed discussions of food supplements—and hence a better understanding of these food products—please see Chapter 6.

One good way in which you can digest more protein than normal is to take digestive enzymes with each meal. A wide variety of these supplements are available in health food stores. We suggest comparing each available digestive enzyme product and purchasing the one that digests fats and carbohydrates as well as protein.

It's also essential to avoid vitamin and mineral deficiencies while attempting to gain weight since any such deficiencies will retard your rate of progress. By taking two or three multipacks of vitamins, minerals, and trace elements each day, you will avoid any progress-stalling nutritional deficiencies. These supplements are best taken with meals, since this practice guarantees optimum assimilation of the nutrients.

Supplemental proteins are an essential part of the weight-gaining diet. It's particularly good to take a protein supplement when you are a little rushed and might miss a scheduled meal. It only takes a couple of minutes to whip up a protein shake in a blender and drink it, and the shake is a superior source of muscle-building protein. See page 61 for Lou Ferrigno's favorite protein shake.

Mike Christian (California Champion) comments on the use of food supplements during an off-season weight-gaining cycle: "It's possible to gain weight without using food supplements, but you won't do it as quickly—nor will you put on as good-quality weight—unless you use food supplements. Digestive enzymes and vitamin/mineral supplements *are* important, but the most vital food supplement during a mass-building cycle is a good-quality protein powder mixed with milk or juice. When I made my biggest surge of growth between 1982 and 1983, I was consuming up to one and a half cups of high-quality protein powder. I'm absolutely convinced that my high-protein diet was an important factor in the gains I made."

IN REVIEW

In this chapter, I've made the following seven key points about weight-gain diet, each of which you should take to heart and combine with a good weight-gain training program:

1. Eat primarily first-class, complete protein from animal sources.
2. Consume no more than 20–30 grams of complete protein at each meal.
3. Eat four to six small, high-protein meals per day.
4. Take digestive enzyme tablets with each meal to facilitate digestion of protein and other nutrients.
5. Use protein supplements, particularly when you will miss or have missed a scheduled meal.
6. Maintain a healthy, balanced diet through the use of vitamins and minerals at mealtimes.
7. Make liberal use of milk and milk products in your diet.

CONCLUSION

The weight-gaining training and nutritional tips I've given you in this chapter *do* work. They've been time-tested and proven by thousands of underweight bodybuilders. But they don't work overnight. Muscular weight gains come slowly in all cases. Only fat gains come quickly, and no one wants to become fat. So be patient. As they say, Rome wasn't built in a day. You won't reach your weight-gain goals in a day either, but you *will* reach them. Go for the gold!

5

CYCLE DIETING

Cycle dieting and its counterpart, cycle training, are secrets of champion bodybuilders that were only recently revealed to the general public. For optimum competitive bodybuilding results you must alternate off-season cycles of training with heavy weights and low reps and precontest cycles of faster, lighter isolation work. And you must alternate off-season nutrition cycles of more relaxed, high-calorie eating with precontest phases of strict caloric control.

Most bodybuilders agree that diet rises in importance in an athlete's training philosophy as a show approaches. **Samir Bannout** (Mr. Universe, Mr. World, and Mr. Olympia) agrees: "Diet is half the battle in bodybuilding, and it rises in importance as you get closer to a competition. The final four to six weeks before a competition, diet is 75 percent of the battle for me. Other bodybuilders might assign slightly different percentages to the importance of diet in our sport, but virtually every champion will agree with me on its great importance."

Cycling your training and diet will greatly increase your longevity in the sport. **Frank Zane** (Mr. America, Mr. Universe, and three-time Mr. Olympia) has competed successfully at the international level for more than 20 years as a result of his intelligent application of the cycling principle of diet and training.

"After each Mr. Olympia, I take a short layoff for a

couple of months," says Zane. "This allows my body to recuperate fully from the all-out training that I did in the weeks and months leading up to the Mr. Olympia. Then my body can rest completely, and any minor injuries I developed during my precontest cycle can heal.

"At the beginning of the new year, I start to get to the gym for more serious training. Over a three or four-month period, I gradually increase the intensity of my training until I reach a moderate peak in the spring. After this, I cut back on my training intensity and begin a second phase, which will result in a summer peak somewhat higher than the spring peak.

"My third peak of the year, the big peak, occurs in the fall for the Mr. Olympia competition. Following my summer peak, I again cut back on the intensity and volume of my workouts, slowly building up to my maximum training intensity.

"I also cycle my diet, making it a little more strict as I reach each relative peak. The combination of cycled training and cycled diet allows me to change the appearance of my body markedly, particularly during the big peak in the fall.

"I'm sure my use of cycle training has contributed to my longevity as a bodybuilder. And, without such longevity, I wouldn't have been able to reach my ultimate degree of development. I've frequently seen bodybuilders train consistently at maximum intensity and diet consistently strictly. They invariably burn out either physically or mentally. Cycle training and diet keep both my body and mind interested in training and responsive to the external stimuli I give them."

THE OFF-SEASON CYCLE

According to **Joe Weider** (publisher of *Muscle & Fitness* magazine and a widely respected trainer of bodybuilding champions), "The heavy workouts you perform in the off-season require high energy levels, so you should adjust your diet to supply these levels of energy. Ordinarily, this requires a diet high in calories, but be careful that you don't eat too many. Male bodybuilders should keep their body weight within six to eight pounds of their competition weight, women within four to five pounds.

"Accumulating body fat makes it difficult to reach sharp competitive condition, and it makes your off-season physical appearance far from an endorsement of bodybuilding. Excessive body fat also weighs you down and decreases your energy levels. Have you ever tried to carry a 30-pound dumbbell around all day? If so, you know what it's like to be 30 pounds overweight."

Samir Bannout agrees that bulking up is foolish: "I don't believe in bulking up. For most bodybuilders, bulking up is simply an excuse to eat like a pig for three or four months. Even in the off-season, my body has grown to crave high-quality foods rather than pizza, cake, cookies, chocolate, and all of the other goodies that used to be so important to me."

Your main objective in the off-season is to increase overall muscle mass, so it's essential that you consume plenty of high-quality protein each day. Virtually all top bodybuilders consume first-class protein from animal sources several times throughout the day.

Sue Ann McKean (California Champion and Superbowl of Bodybuilding Champion) believes, "Maintaining a positive nitrogen balance is essential for muscle mass increases during an off-season training cycle, especially if you experience difficulty in gaining weight. And the best way I know to keep a positive nitrogen balance is to consume small amounts of protein throughout the day.

"I will go ahead and eat a normal three meals per day in the off-season, making sure they are high in protein, and then snack frequently on protein foods the remainder of the day. If I'm going to be on the go all day—which is frequently the case for me—I'll pack cold cuts, hard-boiled eggs, and so forth and take them with me. Whenever I feel even a minor hunger pang, in goes some protein.

"One really good nutritional trick for both off-season and precontest dieting is to carry around desiccated liver tablets and pop four or five of them into your mouth each hour or two, swallowing them with water, juice, or milk.

Not only does this practice help to maintain a positive nitrogen balance, but it also helps to keep your energy levels high for hard and heavy off-season workouts."

In *Muscle & Fitness* magazine, **Joe Weider** reported, "The main dietary supplement for energy production is desiccated liver. In an experiment, scientists fed three groups of lab rats different diets for six weeks. Group One was fed the normal lab rat diet and some liver. Group Two had the same diet but with four times as much liver, and Group Three had the same diet but with *no liver.*

"At the end of the feeding period, each group was placed in a drum of 20-degree (centigrade) water from which they could not escape. They literally were forced to swim or drown, a pure test of muscular endurance. The average endurance time for Group Three (no liver) was 34 minutes; for Group One (a little liver), 38 minutes; and for Group Two (high liver), 69.5 minutes—more than twice that of the no liver group! (A. Ciriaco, 'Increase of Resistance to Stress of Swimming in Cold Water in Rats Given a Diet Rich in Liver,' *Quad Nutrizione*, 1964, 24:289–296. Italian.)."
Italian.)."

One weight-gaining secret used by **Charles Glass** (American and World Middleweight Champion), a self-confessed hard-gainer, is to carry a thermos bottle of protein drink around with him. "I mix it up with whole milk and a milk and egg protein powder in the morning," Charles reveals, "and then take sips of it from time to time at work. I'm an engineer, so it isn't difficult to find time at work to drink a little of my protein every hour or so. This technique requires a fairly large thermos, but it really works wonders. Between winning the World Championships in 1983 and competing in the 1984 Mr. Olympia show, I gained more than 10 pounds of muscular body weight, a record for me."

You might also consider taking free-form amino acid capsules with you to work or school, swallowing three to five of them each hour if possible. This technique was suggested to us by **Matt Mendenhall** (first runner-up, National Championships), who packs a hard 237 pounds of muscle on his 5'11" frame.

"Free-form amino acid capsules are rather expensive, but they are quite effective, making them one of the best supplement investments on the market," says Matt. "If the expense is putting you off, I'd suggest pooling your funds with fellow gym members and buying large quantities of the capsules at wholesale prices. This method can save you up to 50 percent of the total cost of this result-producing food supplement."

Other proven weight-gain methods and suggested diets are outlined in Chapter 4. Be sure to read this chapter and master its information before actually attempting an off-season training and dietary cycle.

Eat more in the off-season, but don't overdo it. Some of the off-season gastronomical feats of champion body-builders are worthy of inclusion in the *Guinness Book of World Records*. Larry Gordon (Mr. Midwest and a Mr. American competition finalist), for example, once ate 37 pieces of chicken in one sitting of only a little more than an hour. The restaurant at which Larry recorded this record had up until that time had an "all the chicken you can eat" policy. PG (post-Gordon), that policy was rescinded.

There have also been many substantiated reports of male bodybuilders eating a gallon of super-rich Haagen Dazs ice cream at a sitting, women eating up to three or four pounds of roast beef at a time, and bodybuilders closing down smorgasbords throughout the land. And, remarkably, the great French bodybuilder Serge Nubret (Mr. World and Mr. Universe) ate an average of nine pounds of meat daily—and mainly horsemeat at that—year in and year out, both off-season and precontest, for more than five years at one point in his career!

TRANSITIONAL PHASES

A valuable recent innovation has been the insertion of short transitional training and dietary cycles between cycles of off-season and precontest intensity. **Joe Weider** notes, "One of the biggest mistakes made by serious bodybuilders is jumping abruptly from an off-season training and nutritional cycle into a precontest regimen. There is such a difference between the intensity levels of these two cycles that a sudden change from an off-season to a precontest phase shocks the body. The results are unnecessary stress and serious problems in maintaining a precontest training and nutritional program.

"If you have been eating 4,000 calories per day in the off-season, you simply can't abruptly drop your daily caloric intake to 1,500–1,800 calories. It's much easier to reduce your intake by 100–200 calories each day or two until you are down to the desired level.

"Moving abruptly from a precontest cycle to an off-season cycle can also cause problems. I've seen bodybuilders, once their contest is behind them, gain 30 pounds in two weeks. Can you imagine what this does to your blood pressure? Additionally, any trained athlete who abruptly ceases physical activity can actually suffer uncomfortable exercise withdrawal symptoms.

"It is clear to me that it's prudent for bodybuilders to insert transitional phases lasting one or two weeks between high-intensity and low-intensity cycles. By making a slower transition between intensity phases, you can gradually induce your body to become accustomed to external training and dietary stimuli, much as you slowly condition your muscles to accept heavier and heavier training loads.

"I am frequently asked—even by highly experienced competitive bodybuilders—how long before a competition a precontest phase should be initiated. This is a highly individual matter, depending on how quickly your body responds and how out of shape you have allowed yourself to become. You can answer this question for yourself through trial and error and by using your training instinct."

THE PRECONTEST CYCLE

You can use a precontest diet either to harden up to evaluate your progress as a bodybuilder or actually to peak for a competition. In either case, you will probably wish to do some aerobic conditioning in addition to dieting, and if you are peaking for a major competition, you will especially need to monitor your sodium intake and—if following a low-fat diet—follow a unique new carbohydrate-loading procedure in order to appear maximally massive, ripped, and vascular onstage.

The type of diet you follow prior to a competition (low-fat/low-calorie, low-carbohydrate, or no diet at all) depends on both your physical and psychological makeup. Most of this book is based on the premise that an individually formulated diet—based on the menus and meal plans in Chapters 7 through 15—will most easily and efficiently eliminate stored fat throughout your body.

When following a low-fat diet, you should begin by eating 3,000 calories per day if you are a man, 1,800 calories per day if you are a woman. Then you progressively reduce your caloric intake as illustrated in the sample meal plans for both men and women in Chapter 14.

The ultimate degree of severity of a precontest diet depends on many factors, but it should not go under 1,500 calories for men and 900 calories for women, because consuming too few calories inevitably results in a loss of muscle mass. Through long experience, champion bodybuilders have discovered that these caloric intake levels are the normal minimums at which it is possible to maintain muscle mass.

Every bodybuilder has a unique metabolic rate. If your metabolism is fast, you need not follow as strict a diet as will someone with a relatively low metabolism. And if you do plenty of aerobic training, you won't need to follow as strict a diet as will someone who does no aerobic workouts. The *only* way to determine how few calories you should consume each day is constantly to monitor your physical appearance in front of a mirror.

It usually takes two or three peaking attempts to master the ability to adjust caloric intake according to your appearance in the mirror. The first time you peak, you will probably misjudge your peak, but a blown peak will give you an idea of correct dietary timing. For example, if you peaked too soon for a competition, you should start your diet closer to the show the next time you decide to peak. And if you failed to peak soon enough for the competition, you will know that you need to begin dieting somewhat earlier.

After two or three peaks, you will know precisely how your body must appear in the mirror at one-week checkpoints leading up to the show, as well as at daily checkpoints the final week prior to a competition. Then, if you are a little ahead of schedule, you can consume a few more calories one day. And if you are behind schedule for your peak, you can consume less food, do more aerobic training, or both in order to put yourself back on schedule.

Some bodybuilders have found that they don't need to diet prior to a competition.

Gladys Portugues, rising young woman bodybuilder, explains: "You know, I have discovered that I really don't need to diet for a competition, at least not the way most bodybuilders do. I have to eat a lot to maintain size. So I'll have hamburgers and shakes and all kinds of food just to keep up my mass. Every person is so different. Each one has to tune in to his or her body to determine what must be done. My battle is keeping it on, not taking it off, and for some reason fat does not form on my body. I happen to have a very high metabolism, and, unlike most women, I have a very low natural fat percentage on my body. One time I foolishly tried out a typical precontest diet. I shrunk down to nothing and even got sick. I was lucky that I even placed."

Regardless of the type of diet you follow, you must be mentally into the peaking process. **Tom Platz** (Mr. Universe) explains: "Your mind controls everything, including how effective a diet is for you. Let me give you an example. For two consecutive competitions, I trained optimally and followed the same diet for the same period of time. For the first competition, I was mentally geared up to appear at my best onstage, and I did peak perfectly. But for the second show, I was mentally distracted by some work at school, and I just couldn't get mentally into the peaking process. As a result, I looked terrible at the second competition. Although I had dieted and trained perfectly, I looked like I hadn't touched a weight and had been feasting for months on jelly doughnuts!"

Steve Michalik (Mr. America) continues this line of reasoning: "The mind is *everything* in dieting. You could be on the right diet and, if you don't believe what you're eating is going to work, it won't work. Also, even if you are *not* eating correctly and your mind believes you are, you can end up looking great onstage. I have a sixth sense for this in myself and other people. I can look at a bodybuilder and instinctively know what he or she needs to consume right up to the day of a show. It's a mystic ability. I always ask the person first about his or her goal. That goes into the computer, and out comes a readout. And I'm invariably able to come up with the right conclusions about what that person should eat. Without a coach, the only way to learn what to eat and not eat is through trial and error."

Aerobic Workouts

Virtually all champion bodybuilders do plenty of aerobic training prior to a competition. According to **Rachel McLish** (twice Miss Olympia and a Pro World Champion), "Low-intensity, prolonged aerobic training is a great way to burn off fat. Physiologically, you simply don't burn fat when involved in the anaerobic type of training usually performed in the gym. All this does is burn up glycogen from the bloodstream, muscles, and liver. In contrast, aerobic exercise actually burns fat as a source of energy, allowing you to lower your body fat levels gradually without necessarily going on such a tight diet that you will lose muscle mass."

Scott Wilson (Pro Mr. America and winner of the Portland Grand Prix competition): "In the off-season, I'll probably do about 30 minutes of aerobics—usually riding my stationary bicycle—three or four times a week. For the last six to eight weeks before a competition, though, I'll do one or two hours of aerobics daily. Typically, I will pedal my bike at a relatively easy pace through one or two hour-long television shows.

"I believe that aerobic workouts—combined with a low-fat/high-carbohydrate diet—are largely responsible for the ability that contemporary bodybuilders have to retain a high degree of muscle mass and attain such a low level of body fat at contest time. Since this emphasis we place on aerobics is relatively new, most bodybuilders still don't appreciate its full importance. As awareness improves, we'll see better and better physiques, even at the novice levels of the sport."

Many bodybuilders, such as **Laura Combes** (the first American Champion in women's bodybuilding), use running for aerobic conditioning. Laura runs three miles in the morning and three or four more in the evening when peaking, and it really works well for her. Very few women in bodybuilding history have been as ripped up as Laura and still had her high degree of muscle mass.

Bodybuilders, particularly the men, are heavier than average, however, and daily running can cause them foot and leg problems. Therefore, cycling and stationary biking, which effectively support your body weight and protect your feet and legs, have become the favorite means of aerobic exercise among champion bodybuilders. **Frank Zane** (three-time Mr. Olympia) is an avid cyclist who even competes in cycling on occasion. And a vast majority of bodybuilders are into stationary cycling, particularly on the new computerized cycles (e.g., Lifecycle) that automatically vary the training intensity during a workout.

Joe Weider has also discovered that it's valuable to increase the number of workouts each day: "This holds true whether these workouts are done in the gym, at aerobic sessions, or at posing practice. You will find that increased daily training frequency elevates the body's BMR [basal metabolic rate], causing your body to burn more fat. Exercise scientists have noted that the body's BMR remains at a higher level for at least an hour after any stiff workout, so more frequent training will keep your metabolism up for more hours each day, resulting in a greater loss of body fat. Therefore, you might profit greatly from a double-split routine followed for a short period of time, as well as from a greater number of aerobic workouts each week."

Sodium Control

Sodium will hold approximately 50 times its weight of

water within the human body, so you *must* carefully monitor sodium intake in the days leading up to a major competition. However, it's not a good idea to start controlling sodium too early in your peaking cycle, since this can actually result in increased water retention.

Frank Zane explains this phenomenon: "If you strictly avoid sodium in your diet for more than a week or so, your body becomes much more sensitive to it, and you'll blow up with water to a greater degree if you accidentally consume some sodium. Your body can flush out excess sodium in only two or three days, so carefully monitoring it for five or six days will be sufficient to eliminate any water retention problems."

Rachel McLish agrees: "Prior to my second Miss Olympia win in 1982, I was eating salty pizza and even drinking margaritas with the salt up to about five days before the show. As a result, my body was holding a lot of water, and people thought I had mistimed my peak and was fat. But as soon as I stopped eating salt, my body began to flush out the excess water it had been holding. On the day of the competition, I was retaining absolutely no water, and I was totally peaked. The rest is history—a second Miss Olympia title."

In order to monitor your sodium intake closely, you will need a nutrition book that lists the sodium content of various foods. One of the best of these books is the *Nutrition Almanac*, which is available in both bookstores and health food stores. It lists the sodium content of virtually any food you might consume in your normal diet.

Carbohydrate Loading

One of the newest techniques of peaking with maximum muscle mass, deep cuts, and plenty of vascularity is to follow a carbohydrate deprivation/loading cycle at the conclusion of a low-fat/high-carbohydrate dietary phase. With this program, you follow a low-carbohydrate diet for at least five to seven days in order to completely deplete your body's carbohydrate stores. This will make you appear flat and a bit smooth, but when this deprivation phase is followed by two or three days of carbohydrate loading, your muscles will appear full and shredded, and your vascularity will be very prominent.

It takes a very strong mind to follow the carbohydrate deprivation/loading schedule because, near the end of the deprivation phase, you will look like you're ready for the undertaker. And your mind will trick you into believing that you have absolutely no chance to win a competition. At this point, many bodybuilders decide not to compete. But if they can stick it out for only a couple more days—realizing that this technique works quite well—they end up onstage in better shape than ever before.

Samir Bannout has done much to popularize the carbohydrate deprivation/loading technique with his articles in *Muscle & Fitness:* "My precontest diet is pretty easy to handle until I reach my carbohydrate deprivation phase about two weeks prior to a competition. Before cutting carbs, I can eat broiled chicken, fish, salads without dressing, baked potatoes, and low-calorie fruit. And I vary my meals from day to day in order to maintain interest in my diet. There's nothing so boring to me as sitting down to eat the same old piece of dry chicken meal after meal.

"When I cut back on the carbs, I eat less than 30 grams of carbohydrate per day for 10 days, which almost turns me into a zombie, particularly for a couple of hours right after I have trained. This hurts like hell, but it's necessary in order for me to look my biggest and most ripped when I go onstage. After the 10 days of carbohydrate deprivation, however, I eat increased amounts of complex carbohydrates for the three days just before my competition. The process is torture, but it works!"

Samir says that he eats some type of complex carbohydrate food (e.g., baked potatoes, vegetables, whole grains) each two hours that he is awake for the last three days before his competition. However, there is a limit to how much carbohydrate you can consume without appearing waterlogged. Try to keep your complex carbohydrate intake down to about one to one and a half grams per pound of body weight per day during the carbohydrate-loading phase.

Strictly avoid the temptation to consume simple sugars

like those found in ice cream and other junk foods when you are carbohydrate loading. They get into your bloodstream too quickly, giving you a blood sugar spike followed by a drastic low point in blood sugar. It's a far better practice to consume complex carbohydrate foods and allow them to give you a low-level but sustained blood sugar flow.

Drugs and Fat Loss

Many bodybuilders take drugs to kill their appetites and to speed up their BMRs prior to a competition, all in an effort to appear more ripped up onstage at a competition. Any use of drugs to reach a bodybuilding peak is a mistake.

Amphetamines, although illegal, are available to kill one's appetite and increase workout energy levels when the going gets tough, but most bodybuilding speed freaks end up appearing stringy, skinny, and unhealthy onstage. These are certainly not qualities of a winner in our sport, so why play around with the drugs? Why not just diet for a longer period of time and eat a few more calories each day? This is a much more sensible plan than using amphetamines.

There are also various thyroid stimulants and supplements that will increase your BMR. This is also a dead end in bodybuilding because your own natural BMR will be suppressed when you are on these drugs. And once you go off them, you will probably blow up like a balloon before your natural BMR can return to normal. Again, it would be a far better practice simply to diet for a longer period of time. It's not unusual to see bodybuilders diet for 10–12 weeks for a major competition. Give it a try!

Robby Robinson.

6
FOOD SUPPLEMENTATION

Food supplementation is one of the most controversial issues in bodybuilding. Opinions on the value of nutritional supplements to bodybuilders vary widely; some bodybuilders use absolutely no supplements, while other champions use literally hundreds of dollars worth of food supplements per month, almost living on these concentrated nutritional products prior to a competition.

Ed Giuliani (Mr. Western America and a Mr. America finalist) confesses, "I spent several years competing quite successfully using absolutely no food supplements and several more years just as successfully using a moderate amount of supplements. To tell you the truth, I felt just as good and made as good gains off supplements as on them."

Dr. Franco Columbu (Mr. World, Mr. Universe, and twice Mr. Olympia) espouses a moderate view of supplementation: "My stand on food supplements is much more moderate than that of most people involved in heavy bodybuilding. One thing I don't often use is a protein supplement. The protein that you get from good food is sufficient for building muscle as long as it contains a good amino acid balance. If you're training hard and eating a lot of meat, fish, poultry, eggs, cheese, and milk, it would be a good idea to help digest the protein by taking hydrochloric acid tablets.

"Vitamins and minerals are far more important to me, but more in the way I take them than in the potencies. You have to have a balanced vitamin and chelated mineral intake. If you take vitamins and *no* chelated minerals, for example, your body will be absorbing and utilizing much less of the vitamins. Only a certain amount of vitamins and minerals is necessary as a catalyst for the body's natural functions.

"The correct combination of vitamins and minerals is vital. It's wrong to inject vitamin B_{12}, for example, as so many bodybuilders do, because all of the B complex elements should be taken together. If you take B_{12}, you become deficient in B_2, and if you take B_6, you become deficient in B_1. And injected vitamins stay in your body for only two hours."

Among the heavier supplement users, especially prior to a show, are two Mr. Olympias, Larry Scott and Frank Zane. Both athletes were associated with the late nutritional guru, Rheo H. Blair, who touted very heavy use of milk and egg protein powder (usually mixed in cream), B complex vitamins, soybean oil extract, and liver extract. Faithfully followed, Blair's complete program of food supplementation costs well over $1,000 per month.

We will discuss all of the more popular food supplements in this chapter, including protein supplements, desiccated liver, kelp, yeast, vitamins, minerals, and trace elements. And we will explain how you can develop a personal nutritional program.

PERSONALIZED NUTRITION

We suggest that you begin your supplementation program by taking only one or two multipacks of vitamins, minerals, and trace elements per day as insurance against progress-halting nutritional deficiencies. These supplements should be taken with your meals for optimum assimilation.

Then, as you grow more experienced as a bodybuilder and develop instinctive training ability (an ability to recognize and interpret the body's biofeedback signals), you can begin to experiment with individual food supplements. Take each individual supplement for at least three or four weeks, carefully noting what effect it has on your body. Then determine if its value outweighs its expense before deciding to add it to your personal nutritional program.

It will take at least a year to determine which individual supplements are of value to you and which are not. But the process will be invaluable to you in the long run. In roughly descending order of importance, we would recommend that you test these individual supplements: amino acids, protein powder, vitamin B complex, the electrolyte minerals (potassium, calcium, and magnesium), vitamin C, desiccated liver, iron, vitamin E, vitamin A, kelp, yeast, each individual B complex vitamin (particularly B_6, B_{12}, and B_{15}), and any other individual vitamins and minerals that can be purchased in a health food store.

PROTEIN SUPPLEMENTS

Bodybuilders go through tons of protein supplements in an effort to force more amino acids into their bloodstreams for use in building an even greater amount of muscle mass. Unfortunately, many bodybuilders waste the money they spend on protein supplements because they are ill informed about how to choose the most effective protein powders, liquids, or capsules.

You don't necessarily get what you pay for at a health food store, because many of the most highly promoted supplements have the advertising costs tacked on to their base price. As a result, the more expensive protein supplements are not necessarily better than some of the less expensive brands. It's a little like buying a new or used car in that you have to do a little bit of investigating and comparison shopping in order to get the best deal.

The concept of using a PER scale to evaluate protein foods was introduced in Chapter 4. The higher the PER, the greater the biological value of a protein food to a bodybuilder. And similarly, the higher the PER of a protein supplement, the more fully it can be used in your diet.

If a protein supplement is lacking in any of the essential amino acids, its PER goes down, and it is of less value to an aspiring bodybuilder. A good case in point is many of the liquid amino acid preparations on the market. Unless fortified with the essential amino acid tryptophan, liquid aminos are almost worthless. They lack this essential amino acid to the point at which the product simply won't help you build significant muscle mass.

Just understanding how liquid amino acids are manu-factured would probably discourage you from using the product. Once the cattle-processing industry has used every part of a steer that's normally edible, the cattle hides and a few unmentionable parts of the animal are left over. But they aren't discarded. Instead, they are placed in large vats and chemically digested to yield their pitiful supply of amino acids. Finally, these aminos—which include very little tryptophan—are concentrated, bottled, and sold. It's little wonder that they taste so ugly.

On the opposite end of the PER scale is the elite form of supplemental protein, free-form amino acid capsules. Free-form aminos contain high concentrations of all the essential amino acids in a form that is readily processed by your digestive system and suffused into your bloodstream. Free-form amino acid capsules are quite expensive, but they are the Porsche of protein supplements. If you can afford them and justify the expense, buy them and use them both with and between meals. And you can espe-cially benefit from using free-form amino acids in the last couple of weeks prior to a competition.

In the middle range of protein supplements are the wide variety of protein powders on the market. Unless you are a strict vegetarian bodybuilder, you should avoid supple-ments that list such low PER items as soybeans, yeast, and sesame seeds in their compilation of ingredients. And since vegetable-source protein concentrates are relatively inex-pensive, they abound in the food supplement industry.

The protein powders consisting purely of powdered egg whites have the highest PER. "It's the only type of protein powder I'll use," states massive **Matt Mendenhall** (National Championships runner-up). However, egg whites are so expensive that even milk-and-egg protein supplements have very little egg content.

Casein, the protein found in milk, is of somewhat lower

biological quality than egg whites but still has a drastically higher PER than any vegetable-source protein. Therefore, a milk-and-egg protein that contains only milk and egg whites will be the best muscle mass-building supplemental powder that you can include in your diet, both from a PER standpoint and in terms of its relative expense per usable gram of each essential and nonessential amino acid.

If you use a pure milk-and-egg protein powder in the range of 90–94 percent protein, you're on the right track in your bodybuilding nutrition program. Then it just boils down to comparing prices for each ounce or pound of the product. If one costs $2 more per pound than a similar product, why buy it?

"Using a milk-and-egg protein powder, you can use the following reliable protein drink recipe," advises **Lou Ferrigno** (Mr. America, Mr. International, twice Mr. Universe and a noted actor):

- 8–10 ounces raw whole milk
- 1 heaping tablespoon protein powder
- 1 banana or other soft fruit for flavoring
- Shaved ice

Directions follow.

"Rather than a banana, you can use a ripe peach or a small handful of strawberries for flavoring. Avoid using chocolate syrup or chocolate drink powder, however, because they have no nutritional value and simply add useless calories to your diet.

"For an optimally blended drink, begin by pouring in the milk and set the blender at a slow speed. Gradually sift in the protein powder until it's completely mixed. Move the blender speed to medium and add the fruit. Finally, add the ice and blend for 30–60 seconds at a high speed to yield a cold, frothy drink. You can even freeze this blend to make a nutritious, tasty, high-protein ice cream!"

A final tip comes from **Sue Ann McKean** (Overall California Champion, Superbowl of Bodybuilding Champion): "You should be careful always to discontinue the use of protein drinks at least two weeks prior to competition because they can tend to bloat your body, obscuring your hard-won muscularity. The consumption of free-form amino acid capsules, however, can safely be continued right up to the day of a competition."

DESICCATED LIVER

In Chapter 5, you were told about a miraculous study in which lab rats fed a great deal of desiccated liver more than doubled their swimming endurance. And yet many bodybuilders who have taken 50–100 desiccated liver tablets per day have noticed no energy increases. Does desiccated liver increase energy or not?

Michael Walczak, MD, a noted bodybuilding nutritionist, comments on the issue: "The problem with this type of experiment is that there are so many variables involved that you can't isolate any of them. It's been postulated that there is a mysterious, unisolated element in liver that causes an increase in endurance.

"I personally feel that it was the protein content in the rats' diet that caused the differences in swimming endurance. A normal lab rat diet is low in protein, so the rats who ate plenty of liver greatly increased the protein content of their diets. Desiccated liver is approximately 70 percent first-class protein, and it contains concentrations of iron and B vitamins.

"My conclusion is that desiccated liver is a fair protein supplement, but it does little, if anything, to increase muscular endurance."

Still, there are numerous bodybuilders—such as Boyer Coe (IFBB Overall Grand Prix Champion, Mr. America, Mr. World, and Mr. Universe) and Frank Zane (Mr. America, Mr. World, Mr. Universe, and three-time Mr. Olympia)— who swear that desiccated liver *does* increase endurance. As recommended earlier in this chapter, you should experiment with using varying amounts of desiccated liver and decide for yourself whether or not the food element increases your endurance.

KELP

Many bodybuilders take tons of kelp tablets, which they

believe to be a good source of minerals—particularly iodine, which supposedly stimulates the thyroid gland to increase the body's BMR and result in a lower body fat level onstage at a competition. However, there is greater evidence that kelp is not what it's cracked up to be as a food supplement.

"Kelp is a very weak source of minerals and is high in sodium, which retains excess water in the body," states Dr. Walczak. "And the iodine in kelp does *not* speed up the metabolism. When a physician encounters a case of hyperthyroidism—too high a metabolism—he will treat the condition by administering Lugol's solution, a suspension of pure iodine!"

BREWER'S YEAST

Many aspiring bodybuilders also consume brewer's yeast as a source of B complex vitamins. But yeast has very low concentrations of B vitamins in comparison to synthetic B complex, and many people are so allergic to yeast that they suffer painfully bloated stomachs whenever they consume it. So, rather than eating brewer's yeast, you should use synthetic B complex vitamins.

ECONOMICAL FOOD SUPPLEMENTATION

Before getting into a detailed discussion of vitamin and mineral supplements, we'd like to give you a few food supplementation tips that can be used if you have a limited budget.

The most economical protein supplement is the powdered milk that you can find in any supermarket. Either add it to regular milk (about one to one and a half tablespoons per glass of milk) or mix it double-strength with water. And if you don't like the taste, you can flavor the resulting drink with any number of flavoring agents. This drink has essentially the same protein content per volume as any protein drink that you would make with milk and egg protein powder, and the amino acid balance is comparable as well.

All types of food supplements can be purchased at up to

50 percent off retail prices by banding together with gym mates and purchasing large quantities at wholesale prices. Most supplement distributors will give you very good discounts when you purchase in large quantities. If you can't find one in your area, we suggest that you write to Ray Riordan, President, Natural Source Products, Inc., PO Box 1285, Canoga Park, CA 91304. Ray has been supplying bodybuilders with quality food supplements for many years and is always happy to sell large quantities of his products at substantial savings to the purchaser.

VITAMINS AND MINERALS

As you will see in the balance of this chapter, there are numerous vitamins, minerals, and trace elements that have a bearing on your health and progress as a serious bodybuilder. In this section, we will discuss the major vitamins and minerals, noting what each nutrient does in your body and where you can obtain that food element in its natural form.

The authors are indebted to Maureen Scott for her research assistance in preparing this chapter. At the time of writing, Ms. Scott was serving as a student intern at *Muscle & Fitness* magazine under the direction of Bill Reynolds, Editor-in-Chief.

Vitamins

Vitamin A (also known as *retinol* or *carotene*) is an unsaturated alcol soluble in fat. Vitamin A is directly involved in the chemistry of the eye and is essential for good vision, particularly at night. Vitamin A is important to bone growth in children and bone replacement in adults. It plays an important role in certain aging processes. In connective tissues, vitamin A increases the permeability of blood capillaries, which in turn contributes to better tissue oxygenation. Vitamin A plays a major role in the health of skin and in the protective activities of mucous membranes throughout the body. Vitamin A is found mainly in mammals and saltwater fish, with a majority of vitamin A supplements consisting of encapsulated fish liver oil. Carotenes, notably the beta-carotene found in leafy green and yellow vegetables and many fruits, can be converted by the body into vitamin A, which can be stored indefinitely in the body's fatty tissues.

Vitamin B complex consists of many individual factors that have a wide-ranging effect on the human body. Most champion bodybuilders use plenty of B complex vitamins, both as a single complex and individually, in their diets. B complex is water-soluble and, as a result, is continually flushed from your body. Therefore, you should take B complex vitamins frequently throughout the day in order to keep sufficient supplies of the vitamin group in your body.

Vitamin B_1 (thiamine) is necessary for glucose reduction, which aids the body in carbohydrate metabolism. This B vitamin is important for lactation, fertility, normal digestion, growth, normal functioning of nerve tissue, and carbohydrate metabolism. Thiamine also helps prevent fatigue, improve circulation, maintain normal red blood cell counts, and increase stamina—functions quite important to athletes. Thiamine can be found naturally in beans, peas, nuts, cereals, brewer's yeast, fresh wheat germ, rice, potatoes, milk, and milk products.

Vitamin B_2 (riboflavin) is needed for the absorption of iron. It is also a coenzyme that makes it possible for the tissue cells of the body to take in oxygen and release wastes. Vitamin B_2 helps the body utilize carbohydrates, fats, and proteins, and a dietary deficiency of this vitamin in the body will most commonly cause anemia. Good natural sources of riboflavin are nuts, beans, sunflower seeds, liver, whole-grain breads, eggs, and milk.

Vitamin B_3 (niacin) is one of the most stable, most easily obtained, and cheapest vitamins required by the human body. It is responsible for dilating the blood vessels and increasing blood flow to the peripheral capillary systems, a function necessary to ensure the healthy functioning of the nervous system. Like riboflavin, niacin is essential to the body's ability to take in and use oxygen. It is also involved in the human body's ability to break down and dispose of excess sugar. Good natural sources of niacin are whole wheat products, sunflower seeds, brown rice, green vegetables, wheat germ, and brewer's yeast.

Vitamin B_5 (pantothenic acid) is important to the following bodily functions: adrenal function, cell building, nervous system health, growth, synthesis of antibodies, conversion of body fat to energy, and the utilization in the human body of choline and PABA, which are discussed later in this section. Good natural sources of pantothenic acid are whole grains, wheat germ, meat, liver, green vegetables, and nuts.

Vitamin B_6 (pyridoxine) comes in three forms: pyridoxine, pyridoxal, and pyridoxamine. All three are used by the body in the same way. Vitamin B_6 is involved mostly in the utilization of protein within the human body, but it's also important in the utilization of fats and carbohydrates. Without B_6, the chemical transformations that our body makes of the food we eat could not take place. B_6 is important in building nerve tissue, muscle tissue, and bone. Good natural sources of pyridoxine are liver, green vegetables, yellow corn, peanuts, tomatoes, bananas, and wheat germ.

Vitamin B_{10} and *vitamin B_{11}* promote muscle and general body growth. They are most easily obtained by taking synthetic B complex vitamin capsules. Good natural sources are whole grains, meat, nuts, and seeds.

Vitamin B_{12} (cobalamin or cyanocobalamin) is required in very small quantities by the human body but is necessary for the normal development of all functioning cells, red blood cells (specifically the bone marrow), the intestines, and the nervous system. Good natural sources of B_{12} are oysters, clams, beef liver, sardines, mackerel, herring, crab, and milk and milk products.

Vitamin B_{13} (orotic acid) is not yet available in individual form in the United States.

Vitamin B_{15} (pangamic acid) is used by many bodybuilders as an antifatigue agent. Most of the studies of B_{15} to date were performed in the Soviet Union. Soviet studies reveal that it can improve blood circulation, stimulate immune responses, improve recovery from fatigue, lower blood cholesterol levels, and protect the organism from environmental pollutants.

Vitamin B_{17} (amygdalin or laetrile) is perhaps the most controversial vitamin of this decade. Chemically composed of two sugar molecules, one benzyaldehyde, and one cyanide called an *amygdalin,* it is known as *nitrilosides* when used in medical doses. B_{17} is made from the pit of an apricot and is the one B vitamin not found in brewer's yeast. It has been purported to have special cancer-controlling and -preventative properties but is still rejected by the FDA on the grounds that it might be harmful due to its cyanide content. Good sources of B_{17} are found in whole kernels of peaches, plums, apricots, nectarines, and apples.

PABA (para-aminobenzoic acid) is one of the newest members of the B complex family. It helps form folic acid and is important in the utilization of protein. PABA has important sunscreening properties and has been proven effective in stopping premature aging. It also helps in the assimilation and effectiveness of pantothenic acid. In animal experiments, it has been combined with pantothenic acid to restore gray hair to its natural color. It also reduces the pain of burns and keeps skin healthy and smooth. Good natural sources of PABA are whole grains, liver, wheat germ, and brewer's yeast.

Choline and *inositol* are lipotrophic agents (fat emulsifiers). They work to help your body utilize fats, particularly cholesterol. Choline is one of the few substances able to penetrate the blood-brain barrier, and it helps the brain produce a chemical that aids the memory. Choline also helps control cholesterol buildups and helps eliminate poisons and drugs from the body via the liver. Good natural sources, of choline and inositol are wheat germ, beef brain, egg yolks, heart, liver, and yeast.

Vitamin C (ascorbic acid) is the least stable of all vitamins. It promotes tissue repair and growth, and it's an important factor in the healing of wounds. Vitamin C prevents fats in the body from turning rancid. It's a natural antibiotic and maintains the strength of blood vessel walls, particularly in the capillary system. Vitamin C is essential to the strength and health of collagen, the "glue" that binds tissues and cells. When used in food as an additive, vitamin C acts as a preservative. It is important in bone and tooth formation, burn healing, and resistance to disease and infection. To overestimate the importance of this vitamin would be impossible. Good natural sources of vitamin C are citrus fruits, acerola cherries, rose hips, turnip greens, strawberries, cantaloupe, and Brussels sprouts.

Vitamin D (calciferol) has one job to do: absorb calcium. It is essential for the activity of vitamin A, and that is why many times supplements contain both of these vitamins in equal amounts. Vitamin D can be synthesized by the human body through the action of sunlight on the skin, but alternative natural sources of vitamin D can be found in cod liver oil, halibut liver oil, egg yolks, and vitamin D-fortified foods such as milk and margarine.

Vitamin E (tocopherol) is essential for a healthy heart and skeletal muscles. As far as athletics is concerned, vitamin E is known as an oxygen conserver and has been found to endow athletes with greater endurance. Vitamin E has been found to be especially valuable for the health of veins in the legs, and it prevents the formation of internal blood clots. Good natural sources of vitamin E are whole wheat, grain oils, almonds, wheat germ, filberts, and peanuts.

Vitamin H (biotin or coenzyme R) is a water-soluble vitamin important to the synthesis of ascorbic acid. Another recent addition to the B complex family, it is essential to normal metabolism of protein and fat by the body. Vitamin H eases muscle pains, aids in keeping hair from graying, alleviates dermatitis and eczema, and is used as a preventative treatment for baldness. Good natural sources of biotin are beef liver, egg yolk, milk, nuts, and fresh fruit.

Vitamin K (menadione) is necessary in that it aids the blood in clotting. It's easily obtained from most vegetables, especially those that have edible green leaves. The best natural sources of vitamin K are cabbage, spinach, cauliflower, beef liver, and egg yolk.

Vitamin M (folic acid or folacin) is water-soluble and is another member of the B complex family. It aids in protein metabolism and is essential to the formation of red blood cells. It has been proven that folic acid must be present in proper quantity in order for division of body cells and production of nucleic acids (RNA and DNA) to take place. It is also needed if sugar and amino acids are to be utilized properly by the body. Folic acid has the ability to act as an analgesic for pain, to promote healthier-looking skin, to help ward off anemia, and to prevent canker sores. Good sources of folic acid are carrots, cantaloupe, avocados, dark rye flour, and liver.

Vitamin P (bioflavonoids) is water-soluble and is composed of rutin, hesperidin, and critrin. It is necessary for the proper function and absorption of vitamin C by the body. The prime function of bioflavonoids is to regulate absorption and increase capillary strength. They aid vitamin C in keeping connective tissues healthy, help build resistance to infection, increase the effectiveness of vitamin C, and help prevent or heal bleeding of the gums. Good natural sources of bioflavonoids are apricots, cherries, rose hips, buckwheat, and the white skin and segments of citrus fruits.

Minerals

Calcium is the mineral responsible for maintaining strong bones and healthy teeth. There is more calcium in the body than any other mineral. It works with magnesium to keep your heart beating regularly. Almost all of the body calcium (two or three pounds of it) is found in the bones and teeth. It helps metabolize your body's iron, alleviates insomnia, and aids the nervous system, especially in the transmission of nerve impulses. It is estimated that 20 percent of an adult's bone calcium is replaced and absorbed each year. To be used effectively by the body, calcium must exist in a two-to-one ratio with phosphorus. The body must also have a sufficient amount of vitamin D in order for calcium to be absorbed. Studies done in America show that calcium and iron are the two minerals most deficient in an American woman's diet. Good natural sources of calcium are milk and milk products, salmon, peanuts, dried beans, and green vegetables.

Iodine (iodide) assists in maintaining a normal body

metabolism. Two-thirds of the body's iodine is found in the thyroid gland. Since the thyroid gland is responsible for controlling metabolism, and iodine influences the thyroid function, a deficiency or excess of the mineral can cause lack of energy, slow mental action, and weight gain. Iodine is important because it improves mental alacrity; gives you more energy; promotes growth of healthy hair, nails, skin, and teeth; and can help you with dieting by burning excess fat. Good natural sources of iodine are all seafoods, kelp, and onions.

Iron is a mineral essential to the production of red blood corpuscles (hemoglobin), red pigment in the blood (myoglobin), and certain enzymes. Studies show that only 8 percent of our iron intake is absorbed and actually utilized in the bloodstream. It has also been shown that iron and calcium are the two major dietary deficiencies in American females' diets. Iron is important in that it promotes resistance to disease, prevents fatigue, aids growth, prevents and cures iron-deficiency anemia. Good natural sources of iron are heart and liver, raw clams, red meat, peaches, oysters, egg yolks, and nuts.

Magnesium is essential to calcium and vitamin C metabolism as well as metabolism of potassium, sodium, and phosphorus. It is also important to converting blood sugar into energy and is essential to effective nerve and muscle function. It is sometimes called "the antistress mineral," and alcoholics are found to be the group most commonly deficient in magnesium. Magnesium has been shown to be effective in fighting depression, keeping teeth healthy, promoting a healthy cardiovascular system, and preventing calcium deposits, kidney stones, and gallstones. Good natural sources of magnesium are nuts, dark green vegetables, apples, grapefruit, lemons, seeds, and figs.

Phosphorus is a mineral found in every cell of the body. In order for it to function effectively, vitamin D and calcium must be in proper proportion, and twice as much calcium as phosphorus should be present so that phosphorus can aid the kidneys in functioning, regulate the heart, and assist in the transfer of nerve impulses. Phosphorus is necessary to normal tooth and bone development, and niacin cannot be assimilated without phosphorus. Phosphorus has been shown to promote healthy gums and teeth, lessen the pain of arthritis, aid in growth and body repair, and provide energy by assisting in the metabolism of fats and starches. Good natural sources of phosphorus are eggs, poultry, fish, and whole grains.

Manganese is essential for healthy, strong connective tissues. Good natural sources of manganese are seeds, nuts, and whole grains.

Zinc is the mineral that is essential to protein synthesis. It aids in the formation of insulin, oversees the contractibility of muscles, is important as a blood stabilizer, maintains an acid-alkaline balance in the body, and is important in the development of all reproductive organs. Zinc is also important because it accelerates healing time for both internal and external injuries, is used as a treatment for infertility, promotes growth and mental alertness, and aids in reduction of cholesterol deposits in the vascular system. Good natural sources of zinc are brewer's yeast, eggs, round steak, pork loin, and lamb chops.

Trace minerals (trace elements) such as cobalt, chromium, and molybdenum are substances the body needs in small quantities. The best way for athletes to prevent trace mineral deficiencies is to adhere to a diet rich in fresh fruit and seafood and to take supplemental kelp tablets.

Candy Csencstis.

7

VEGETABLE DISHES

Vegetables are among the most delightful foods available to bodybuilders. They are low in calories, appealing to the eye, and satisfying to the digestive system. They provide much-needed vitamins, minerals, and, of great importance, roughage.

When you have eaten your food allotment for the day, say in protein and fat, and you face the long hours until the next morning with little or nothing left that is "allowed," vegetables come to the rescue.

This is true because vegetables are so low in calories that it would not make a great deal of difference if you "splurged" and had, say, Asparagus Frittata or Broccoli Boufant.

The recipes in this chapter are designed to add variety and excitement to your bodybuilding diet, even up to and including those terrible final days before contest date.

Be aware that you can switch vegetables for a given recipe and come up with a dish that might be more suitable for or appealing to you. For example, there is no reason why you can't change Asparagus Fatburners to String Bean Fatburners or Cauliflower Fatburners if either of those vegetables happens to appeal to you or agrees with your body more than the listed vegetable. Be creative with the recipes.

The recipes in this chapter are grouped by the main vegetable used.

ASPARAGUS

ASPARAGUS FATBURNERS

1 bunch fresh asparagus   ¼ cup lemon juice
Water   2 tablespoons parsley

1. Trim off scales and ends of asparagus; wash trimmed spears.
2. Tie asparagus in bunches and stand upright in double boiler.
3. Add 3 inches of water and invert top of boiler to serve as a cover, so that the tops of the asparagus will steam while the bottoms boil.
4. Cook asparagus until tender and remove from water. Cut strings.
5. Arrange on platter and pour lemon juice and parsley over asparagus.

Serves 4

Per serving: 9.5 calories, 1 gram protein, 2 grams carbohydrate, 0 grams fat.

ASPARAGUS FRITTATA

1 8-ounce can chopped asparagus
1 tablespoon finely chopped scallion
1 tablespoon chopped green pepper
4 egg whites
2 tablespoons low-fat cottage cheese
1½ teaspoons skim milk
1 teaspoon parsley
⅓ teaspoon pepper

1. Drain asparagus. Pour 3 teaspoons of asparagus liquid into nonstick skillet.
2. Chop asparagus into small pieces and add to skillet.
3. Add scallions and green pepper.
4. Cook over low heat until green peppers are tender.
5. Beat egg whites with a fork until frothy and stir them into cottage cheese. Add skim milk, parsley, and

pepper. Mix until smooth.
6. Pour cheese mixture over vegetables in skillet and stir well.
7. Cook over low heat until bottom is slightly brown.
8. Turn over and brown other side.
9. Bake in a 300°F oven for 15 minutes. Cut into wedges and serve.

Serves 2

Per serving: 83 calories, 12 grams protein, 8 grams carbohydrate, 0.5 grams fat.

BROCCOLI
BROCCOLI BOUFANT

1 small onion, chopped
Water
1 10-ounce package chopped broccoli, cooked
12 egg whites, beaten stiff
½ teaspoon garlic powder
Dash pepper
½ cup skim milk
½ cup grated Parmesan cheese

1. Simmer onion in ½ inch water in a nonstick skillet.
2. Cover onion with broccoli.
3. Combine stiffly beaten egg whites with garlic powder and pepper.
4. Add milk and beat again.
5. Pour mixture over broccoli and onion and stir. Cook over medium heat for 5 minutes.
6. Sprinkle with Parmesan cheese. Cook another 5 minutes over medium heat.
7. Cut into wedges.
8. Serve immediately.

Serves 4

Per serving: 147 calories, 19 grams protein, 10 grams carbohydrate, 3 grams fat.

CREAMED BROCCOLI SOUP

1 10-ounce package frozen chopped broccoli
1 small onion, sliced
1 whole clove
⅛ teaspoon pepper
2 cups water
1 tablespoon cornstarch
2 cups skim milk

1. Place broccoli, onion, clove, pepper, and water in a pot and cook, covered, until broccoli is very tender.
2. Remove clove and place broccoli mixture in blender.
3. Blend for 2 minutes until pureed and place mixture in pot again.
4. In a bowl, combine cornstarch and milk and stir into a paste.
5. Stir paste into broccoli mixture.
6. Heat, stirring constantly, until broccoli mixture is thickened into a bisque-type stew.

Serves 4

Per serving: 89 calories, 8 grams protein, 15 grams carbohydrate, 0.5 grams fat.

CARROTS
CARACO CARROTS AND APPLESAUCE

1 pound frozen baby carrots
1 8-ounce can crushed pineapple (water-packed, drained)
1 1-pound can unsweetened applesauce
2 teaspoons ground cinnamon
¼ teaspoon ground ginger
2 teaspoons lemon juice

1. Combine all ingredients in a bowl and mix.
2. Place mixture in a small nonstick baking pan.
3. Bake in a 350°F oven for 20 minutes.

Serves 4

Per serving: 147 calories, 1.7 grams protein, 37.3 grams carbohydrate, 0.7 grams fat.

VEGETABLE CUTLETS

¾ cup water
1 cup chopped onion
½ cup chopped celery
1 cup grated carrots
½ cup green beans (fresh or frozen)
½ cup green peas (frozen)
½ cup water
2 egg whites, beaten stiff
¼ teaspoon pepper
4 tablespoons whole wheat bread crumbs (*see* index)

1. Bring water to boil in nonstick skillet.
2. Add onion, celery, and carrots and cook for 35 minutes.
3. Add beans and peas and ½ cup water.
4. Cook until vegetables are tender.
5. Add beaten egg whites and mix well.
6. Add pepper and bread crumbs.
7. Shape into patties and bake at 400°F in a nonstick baking dish for 20 minutes.

Serves 4

Per serving: 85.5 calories, 5 grams protein, 17 grams carbohydrate, 0.4 grams fat.

CAULIFLOWER
FAT-FREE CAULIFLOWER POLONAISE

1 head cauliflower
2 egg whites, hard-boiled and chopped
3 tablespoons chopped fresh parsley
3 tablespoons toasted whole wheat bread crumbs

1. Boil or steam cauliflower until tender. Place on serving plate.
2. Combine egg whites with parsley and bread crumbs.
3. Sprinkle egg white mixture on cauliflower and serve.

Serves 4

Per serving: 34 calories, 4 grams protein, 5.6 grams carbohydrate, 0.2 grams fat.

EGGPLANT
EGGPLANT-ZUCCHINI MEDLEY

1 eggplant, peeled and diced
3 zucchini, sliced
2 green peppers, diced
1 onion, sliced thin
1 clove garlic, minced
2 large tomatoes, cut into ½-inch strips
½ teaspoon oregano
¼ teaspoon pepper

1. Combine all ingredients in large, heavy pot.
2. Cook, covered, for 20 minutes over low heat.
3. Uncover and cook for 15 minutes over moderate heat, stirring occasionally to prevent burning.

Serves 4

Per serving: 78 calories, 4 grams protein, 13.6 grams carbohydrate, 0.5 grams fat.

EASY EGGPLANT PARMESAN

1 large eggplant
Water
1 28-ounce can tomato puree
1 tablespoon oregano
1 pound low-fat cottage cheese
¼ teaspoon oregano
1 clove garlic, crushed
2 tablespoons whole wheat flour
4 ounces low-fat mozzarella cheese, grated
2 tablespoons grated Parmesan cheese
¼ teaspoon garlic powder

1. Slice eggplant into ½-inch rounds and place in ½ inch water in vegetable steamer.
2. Steam for 10 minutes while heating tomato puree with 1 tablespoon oregano in another pot.
3. Mix cottage cheese with ¼ teaspoon oregano, garlic, and flour.
4. Place a layer of eggplant, then a layer of cottage cheese, then tomato sauce in a baking dish. Repeat layers until all ingredients have been used.
5. Top with grated mozzarella and grated Parmesan cheese.
6. Bake uncovered in a 350°F oven for 20 minutes.

Serves 4

Per serving: 305 calories, 29 grams protein, 31 grams carbohydrate, 8 grams fat.

EGGPLANT PARMIGIANA

½ pound very lean ground beef
½ teaspoon onion powder
¼ teaspoon garlic powder
1 28-ounce can salt-free tomatoes
1 6-ounce can tomato paste
½ teaspoon oregano
1 teaspoon dried basil
1 large eggplant
¼ cup sapsago cheese

1. Cook ground beef in nonstick frying pan until brown.
2. Sprinkle with garlic and onion powders and stir well.
3. Add tomatoes, tomato paste, oregano, and basil.
4. Cook, covered, for 15 minutes.
5. Peel eggplant and slice into ¼-inch slices.
6. Spread a layer of beef mixture to cover the bottom of a nonstick baking dish. Top with layer of eggplant.
7. Repeat layers, ending with beef mixture, and sprinkle with grated sapsago cheese.
8. Bake in a 350°F oven for 40 minutes.

Serves 4

Per serving: 204 calories, 18 grams protein, 20 grams carbohydrate, 6 grams fat.

GREEN BEANS
STRING BEAN AND MUSHROOM COMBO

1 medium onion, chopped fine
½ pound fresh mushrooms, sliced
Water
½ pound fresh green beans, cut into 2-inch pieces
⅛ cup water
Dash pepper

1. Simmer onion and mushrooms in ½ inch of water in a nonstick skillet.

2. Add green beans and ⅛ cup water. Sprinkle with pepper.
3. Cover and cook for 15 minutes.

Serves 2

Per serving: 69 calories, 5 grams protein, 13 grams carbohydrate, 0.5 gram fat.

GREEN BEANS AND TOMATOES OREGANNATO

1 pound fresh green beans, trimmed and cut into 3-inch pieces
2 fresh tomatoes, chopped
1 small onion, diced
½ teaspoon oregano
⅛ teaspoon pepper
1 cup water

1. Place green beans, tomatoes, onion, oregano, pepper, and water in small pot.
2. Cook until beans are tender-crisp (10 minutes).
3. Drain and serve.

Serves 4

Per serving: 39 calories, 8.6 grams protein, 2 grams carbohydrate, 0 grams fat.

SPINACH

POWER WORKOUT SPINACH AND COTTAGE CHEESE

½ 10-ounce package chopped spinach
1 scallion, sliced thin
1/3 teaspoon ground nutmeg
Water
½ cup low-fat cottage cheese
¼ teaspoon oregano
⅛ teaspoon rosemary

1. Cook spinach, scallion, and nutmeg in a small amount of water in a pot over a medium flame for 5 minutes.
2. Drain and spread mixture in bottom of a small baking dish.
3. Top with cottage cheese mixed with oregano and rosemary.
4. Bake in a 350°F oven for 15 minutes.

Serves 1

Per serving: 114 calories, 16.7 grams protein, 6.6 grams carbohydrate, 2 grams fat.

SPINACH AND CHEESE PIE

Water
1 pound fresh spinach, trimmed
1 pound skim-milk ricotta cheese
¾ cup grated low-fat cheddar cheese
6 egg whites, beaten
½ teaspoon pepper
½ teaspoon garlic powder
½ cup sliced mushrooms

1. Preheat oven to 350°F.
2. Place ¼ inch water in a pot, place a vegetable steamer in pot, and add spinach.
3. Cover pot and steam for 2 minutes.

4. Remove spinach and cut into small pieces. Mix with remaining ingredients.
5. Pour into a small nonstick baking dish and bake for 35 minutes.

Serves 2

Per serving: 616 calories, 55.7 grams protein, 24 grams carbohydrate, 13 grams fat.

POPEYE'S PLATTER

1 pound fresh spinach   1 tablespoon vegetable oil
1 clove garlic, crushed

1. Wash spinach and remove stems. Drain.
2. Heat oil and garlic in nonstick skillet.
3. Add spinach and stir.
4. Cook for 1 minute over high heat.
5. Uncover and cook 2 minutes more, stirring.

Serves 4

Per serving: 59 calories, 3.6 grams protein, 5 grams carbohydrate, 3.9 grams fat.

TOMATOES
DILL-GRILLED TOMATOES

4 medium tomatoes   2 tablespoons dried dill
¼ teaspoon pepper   1 teaspoon grated cheese

1. Arrange tomatoes in a nonstick baking dish.
2. Cut a cross in the top of each tomato and sprinkle inside of tomato with pepper, dill weed, and cheese.
3. Place tomatoes under broiler for 10 minutes or until tomatoes are heated through.

Serves 4

Per serving: 35 calories, 2 grams protein, 7 grams carbohydrate, 0.4 grams fat.

ZUCCHINI

GLUTEUS MINIMUS ZUCCHINI STEW

1 large zucchini, diced
1 medium onion, chopped
1 medium green pepper, chopped
1 medium tomato, chopped
1 teaspoon oregano
1 teaspoon dried basil
1 teaspoon chili powder
1 teaspoon garlic powder
½ cup water

1. Mix all ingredients in a saucepan with water.
2. Cover and simmer for 1 hour.

Serves 4

Per serving: 27 calories, 1 gram protein, 4.6 grams carbohydrate, 0 grams fat.

ZESTY ZUCCHINI STEW

2 medium zucchini, sliced ¼ inch thick
6 tomatoes, cut into eighths
½ cup water
1 small onion, sliced thin
1 tablespoon dried parsley flakes
¼ teaspoon thyme
⅛ teaspoon black pepper

1. Place zucchini, tomatoes, water, and onion in a pot.
2. Add parsley, thyme, and pepper.
3. Cover and cook for 15 minutes.

Serves 4

Per serving: 66 calories, 3.3 grams protein, 12 grams carbohydrate, 0.5 grams fat.

BAKED ZUCCHINI AND CHEESE CASSEROLE

8 slices protein bread, cubed
1 medium zucchini, sliced thin
½ cup grated Parmesan or Romano cheese
1½ cups skim milk
4 egg whites, beaten
1 teaspoon dried basil
¾ teaspoon thyme
½ teaspoon dry mustard
⅛ teaspoon pepper

1. Preheat oven to 350°F
2. Arrange bread cubes in a 9-inch pie plate or small baking dish.
3. Top cubes with zucchini and sprinkle with grated cheese.
4. Beat together egg whites, milk, and all seasonings.
5. Pour over bread and cheese mixture.
6. Bake for 40 minutes and serve immediately.

Serves 4

Per serving: 192 calories, 18 grams protein, 20 grams carbohydrate, 3 grams fat.

PARMESAN ZUCCHINI

2 zucchini
Water
¼ cup grated Parmesan cheese
2 tablespoons chopped fresh parsley

1. Slice zucchini into very thin slices.
2. Simmer zucchini slices in ½ inch water in a nonstick skillet.
3. Drain.
4. Spread mixture evenly onto nonstick baking sheet and sprinkle with Parmesan cheese and parsley.
5. Bake in a 350°F oven for 20 minutes.

Serves 4

Per serving: 37 calories, 3 grams protein, 0.6 grams carbohydrate, 1.5 grams fat.

STUFFED ZUCCHINI

3 large zucchini
1 onion, sliced thin
1 green pepper, diced
1 clove garlic, minced
½ cup chopped fresh tomatoes
1 cup tomato juice
1 teaspoon oregano
1 slice whole wheat toast

1. Cut zucchini in half lengthwise and remove pulp, leaving ½-inch-thick shells. Save shells for stuffing.
2. Dice scooped-out zucchini and place in large nonstick skillet with onion, green pepper, garlic, and tomatoes. Add ¼ cup of the tomato juice and the oregano.
4. Cook until vegetables are limp.
5. Fill reserved zucchini shells with mixture and arrange in nonstick baking dish.
6. Pour remaining tomato juice over stuffed zucchini.

7. Crumble toast and sprinkle on top of zucchini.
8. Bake in a 350°F oven for 30 minutes.
9. Serve with tomato juice gravy spooned over zucchini.

Serves 4

Per serving: 66 calories, 3 grams protein, 10.5 grams carbohydrate, 0.4 gram fat.

Samir Bannout.

8

SALAD DISHES

There are all kinds of exciting salads in this chapter. They range from those consisting mainly of vegetables to those consisting for the most part of fruit. What they all have in common, however, is that they are an excellent source of complex carbohydrates.

Salads provide the bodybuilder with vitamins, minerals, and roughage. They also provide the often dehydrated bodybuilder with a source of water. Lettuce, for example, is 97 percent water.

Because of their bulk and roughage, they tend to satisfy the appetite without adding lots of calories to your diet. What is more, they allow for all sorts of creativity. You will see that in this section we have mixed and matched all sorts of unusual combinations. We hope that you will be inspired to take some chances yourself and mix and match still more exotic combinations.

We have also included one of the most vital necessities for a good salad—a variety of dressings, all of them very low in calories and fat. Dressings run the gamut from Russian, French, and Italian to Easy Orange and Apple Wine. The dips that end the chapter can be used either as salad dressings or as dips to serve with raw vegetables. Never again will you, as a bodybuilder, have to look forward with dread to that same old "lettuce and vinegar" salad.

You may want to create your own dressings by adding

various spices to plain vinegar. Simply experiment with the spice and herb list given in Chapter 2.

FRUIT SALADS
ORANGE-CRESS SALAD

2 oranges, peeled and sliced
1 small bunch watercress, washed and trimmed
½ cup evaporated skim milk
2 tablespoons lemon juice
½ teaspoon dried dill

1. Arrange orange slices and watercress on 2 plates.
2. Combine evaporated skim milk, lemon juice, and dill.
3. Pour dressing over salad and serve.

Serves 2

Per serving: 89 calories, 3.7 grams protein, 19.5 grams carbohydrate, 0.4 grams fat.

ORANGE AND CAULIFLOWER SUPERSET SALAD

2 10½-ounce cans unsweetened mandarin orange
    segments, drained
2 cups uncooked cauliflower pieces
¼ cup chopped green pepper
2 cups chopped spinach leaves
¼ cup white vinegar
1 teaspoon lemon juice
¼ teaspoon onion powder
¼ teaspoon oregano

1. Toss orange segments, cauliflower pieces, green pepper, and spinach together in a bowl.
2. Mix vinegar with lemon juice, onion powder, and oregano.
3. Pour dressing over salad ingredients and toss again.
4. Chill and serve.

Serves 4

Per serving: 70 calories, 16.5 grams protein, 3 grams carbohydrate, 0.4 grams fat.

COCONUT-PEACH SALAD

⅓ cup low-fat cottage cheese
1 tablespoon chopped dry-roasted peanuts
1 tablespoon chopped maraschino cherries, drained
1 fresh peach, halved
2 tablespoons flaked coconut
Lettuce leaves
Lemon juice to taste

1. Mix cottage cheese, peanuts, and cherries together.
2. Fill centers of peach halves with cottage cheese mixture.
3. Sprinkle with coconut.
4. Arrange on lettuce leaves and sprinkle with lemon juice.

Serves 2

Per serving: 112 calories, 12 grams protein, 7 grams carbohydrate, 4.4 grams fat.

TOMATO-PINEAPPLE VINAIGRETTE

1 8-ounce can sliced pineapple (water-packed)
1 tomato, sliced
1 green pepper, cut into strips
Lettuce
½ cup vinegar (any kind)

1. Divide pineapple slices between 2 lettuce leaves.
2. Place tomato slices and pepper strips on top of pineapple.
3. Pour vinegar over salads and serve.

Serves 2

Per serving: 71 calories, 2 grams protein, 17 grams carbohydrate, 0.5 grams fat.

SIX FRUITS SALAD

1 apple, chopped
1 orange, diced
¼ banana, cut into small pieces (chiplike)
2 slices pineapple, chopped
5 strawberries, chopped
¼ cantaloupe, cut into small pieces (chiplike)

1. Combine all ingredients in mixing bowl. Toss.
2. Chill and serve with a salad dressing (*See* index).

Per serving: 205 calories, 2.2 grams protein, 52 grams carbohydrate, 1.6 grams fat.

VEGETABLE SALADS
MARINATED STRING BEANS

½ cup cooked green beans
1 tablespoon tarragon vinegar
¼ tablespoon dried dill
Dash garlic powder
1 tablespoon orange juice

1. Place green beans in plastic container.
2. Combine tarragon vinegar, dill weed, garlic powder, and orange juice in a small bowl.
3. Pour liquid over string beans in container and cover.
4. Refrigerate beans for 3 hours or overnight.
5. Serve on a bed of lettuce.

Serves 1

Per serving: 24.5 calories, 1 gram protein, 5.5 grams carbohydrate, 0 grams fat.

EASY SPINACH SALAD

6 fresh spinach leaves, trimmed
1 (hard-boiled) egg white, chopped
⅛ teaspoon garlic powder

Dash pepper
2 tablespoons tarragon vinegar
1 tablespoon water

1. Arrange spinach leaves on a dinner plate.
2. Sprinkle with egg white.
3. Stir together garlic powder, pepper, vinegar, and water.
4. Pour dressing over salad and serve.

Serves 1

Per serving: 31 calories, 5 grams protein, 2.7 grams carbohydrate, 0.2 grams fat.

RED PEPPER SALAD

1 head lettuce
1 sweet red pepper
½ cup tomato juice (unsalted)
2 tablespoons nonfat yogurt
1 tablespoon lemon juice
¼ teaspoon garlic powder

1. Wash, dry, and tear lettuce into small pieces. Place lettuce in salad bowl.
2. Remove seeds from pepper and cut into long strips. Add to lettuce.
3. Pour tomato juice, yogurt, lemon juice, and garlic powder into electric blender. Blend at medium speed until mixture is smooth and pour over salad.

Serves 4

Per serving: 51 calories, 3 grams protein, 10.4 grams carbohydrate, 0.5 grams fat.

NADIA'S ROMAINE LETTUCE SALAD

1 head romaine lettuce
1 small red onion, sliced thin
¼ cup tarragon vinegar
2 tablespoons water

2 tablespoons lemon juice
¼ teaspoon dry mustard
Dash pepper

1. Tear lettuce into pieces and place in salad bowl.
2. Add onion.
3. Combine vinegar, water, lemon juice, mustard, and pepper and mix.
4. Pour over lettuce and onion and serve.

Serves 4

Per serving: 25.5 calories, 1.4 grams protein, 4.3 grams carbohydrate, 0.3 grams fat.

SPINACH-MUSHROOM SALAD

1 pound fresh spinach
¼ pound fresh mushrooms
1 egg white, hard-boiled
¼ cup tarragon vinegar
2 tablespoons water
⅛ teaspoon pepper
⅛ teaspoon paprika
1 tablespoon undiluted frozen orange juice concentrate

1. Trim and wash spinach and place in salad bowl.
2. Wash and slice mushrooms and add to spinach.
3. Combine vinegar, water, pepper, paprika, and orange juice concentrate.
4. Pour dressing over salad.

Serves 2

Per serving: 46.3 calories, 4.3 grams protein, 5 grams carbohydrate, 0.3 grams fat.

BIG FELLA'S TRAVEL SPINACH SALAD

8 ounces fresh spinach
1 small head lettuce, washed and chilled
2 teaspoons lemon juice
¼ cup vinegar (any kind)
2 tablespoons water
½ teaspoon dried dill
½ teaspoon dry mustard
½ teaspoon chopped fresh parsley
Dash pepper
Dash garlic powder

1. Wash spinach, remove stems, and dry leaves. Tear spinach leaves and lettuce into small pieces and place in salad bowl.
2. Place lemon juice, vinegar, water, dill, mustard, parsley, pepper, and garlic powder in small pot and heat until just ready to boil.
3. Pour over spinach, toss, and serve immediately.

Serves 4

Per serving: 21 calories, 2 grams protein, 4 grams carbohydrate, 0.2 grams fat.

DILLED TOMATOES AND ONIONS

2 large tomatoes, sliced thick
1 large Bermuda onion, sliced thin
2 tablespoons chopped fresh dill
Splash wine vinegar

1. Arrange sliced tomatoes and onions on a platter.
2. Sprinkle fresh dill over vegetables.
3. Splash on vinegar and serve.

Serves 2

Per serving: 27.6 calories, 2.6 grams protein, 12.5 grams carbohydrate, 1.8 grams fat.

ZESTY CUCUMBER SALAD

1 large cucumber, peeled and sliced thin
1 white onion, sliced thin
½ cup white vinegar
¼ cup wine vinegar
¼ cup water
1 tablespoon dried dill
1 tablespoon undiluted frozen apple juice concentrate, thawed
¼ tablespoon pepper

1. Combine cucumber and onion in a small deep bowl.
2. Combine vinegars, water, dill, apple juice concentrate, and pepper. Mix well and pour over cucumbers.
3. Keep salad in refrigerator 24 hours before serving. Mix from time to time. (You may serve before, but the full flavor will not have developed yet.)

Serves 2

Per serving: 27.9 calories, 1.1 grams protein, 6.4 grams carbohydrate, 0.1 grams fat.

SPINACH-CUCUMBER-MUSHROOM TRISETS

1 medium cucumber, sliced thin
½ cup vinegar
⅛ teaspoon oregano
⅛ teaspoon dried basil
⅛ teaspoon thyme
⅛ teaspoon dried bell pepper
Dash onion powder
Dash garlic powder
10 ounces fresh spinach
½ cup sliced fresh mushrooms
3 egg whites, hard-boiled and sliced

1. Place cucumber slices in bowl.
2. Mix vinegar with oregano, basil, thyme, dried bell pepper, onion powder, and garlic powder.

3. Pour vinegar mixture over cucumber slices in bowl.
4. Refrigerate mixture for 1 hour.
5. Wash spinach, removing stems, and place in salad bowl, tearing leaves into small pieces.
6. Pour cucumber slices with dressing over spinach and add mushroom slices.
7. Toss and add egg whites. Serve chilled.

Serves 4

Per serving: 36 calories, 2.7 grams protein, 9 grams carbohydrate, 0.3 grams fat.

GARDEN MUSHROOM-BEAN SALAD

1 head romaine lettuce, washed and chilled
1 head iceberg lettuce, washed and chilled
½ pound mushrooms, stemmed and sliced
1 cup cooked string beans

1. Line salad bowl with romaine lettuce leaves.
2. Tear iceberg lettuce into small pieces and add to bowl.
3. Add mushrooms and string beans and toss lightly.
4. Serve with Garden Dressing (*See* index).

Serves 6–8

Per serving: 40 calories, 3.2 grams protein, 7.4 grams carbohydrate, 0.4 grams fat.

CHILI WILLIE SALAD

1 medium onion, sliced thin
1 cup coarsely chopped green pepper
2 cups coarsely chopped fresh tomato
¼ cup wine vinegar
1 teaspoon chili powder
2 drops red pepper sauce

1. Separate onion slices into rings.
2. Place onion rings, green pepper, and tomato in large bowl.
3. Stir vinegar, chili powder, and red pepper sauce together. Pour over vegetables and toss.
4. Chill and serve.

Serves 4

Per serving: 37.5 calories, 1.8 grams protein, 8 grams carbohydrate, 0.7 grams fat.

BRUSSELS SPROUT AND TOMATO SALAD

2 10-ounce packages frozen Brussels sprouts
¾ cup garlic-flavored wine vinegar
½ teaspoon chives
½ pint cherry tomatoes
4 large lettuce leaves

1. Cook Brussels sprouts according to directions.
2. Pour vinegar mixed with chives over Brussels sprouts.
3. Cool for 2 hours in refrigerator.
4. Cut cherry tomatoes in half and add to Brussels sprout mixture.
5. Toss and place on lettuce leaves.

Serves 4

Per serving: 37 calories, 3 grams protein, 7 grams carbohydrate, 0.3 grams fat.

THREE-BEAN SALAD

1 16-ounce can kidney beans
1 16-ounce package frozen wax beans, cooked
1 16-ounce package frozen green beans, cooked
6 mushrooms, chopped
½ cup cider vinegar
¼ cup salad oil
¼ cup chopped onion

1. Drain kidney beans and place in bowl with cooked wax and green beans. Add mushrooms.
2. Add vinegar, oil, and onion and toss.
3. Refrigerate until ready to serve.

Serves 4

Per serving: 271 calories, 9.3 grams protein, 28.8 grams carbohydrate, 14.8 grams fat.

SALAD DRESSINGS AND DIPS
CREAMY FRUIT SALAD DRESSING

¾ cup low-fat yogurt (any flavor)
¼ cup orange juice
Dash ground cinnamon
Dash ground nutmeg
¼ teaspoon grated orange rind
1 tablespoon dry white wine

1. Combine all ingredients in bowl.
2. Mix well or beat lightly.
3. Chill and serve.

Serves 4

Per serving: 37 calories, 2 grams protein, 5 grams carbohydrate, 0.7 grams fat.

EASY ORANGE DRESSING

7 ounces evaporated skim milk
3 ounces undiluted frozen orange juice concentrate, thawed

1. Place evaporated milk and orange juice concentrate in blender.
2. Blend on low speed for 1 minute.
3. Pour into jar and use as salad dressing.

Serves 8; makes 1 cup

Per serving: 10.4 calories, 0.5 grams protein, 2 grams carbohydrate, 0.03 grams fat.

HERBED VINEGAR DRESSING

¾ cup wine vinegar
¼ cup fresh dill *or* ½ teaspoon dried dill
¼ cup fresh snipped chives
1/3 cup fresh snipped mint
1 clove garlic, chopped fine
⅛ teaspoon chopped fresh parsley

1. Combine all ingredients.
2. Let dressing remain refrigerated in plastic container for 5 days.
3. Strain and remove herbs.
4. Serve over lettuce or any salad.

Serves 8; makes 1 cup

Per serving: 2 calories, 0.1 grams protein, 0.4 grams carbohydrate, 0 grams fat.

TOMATO-LEMON DRESSING

½ cup tomato juice
2 tablespoons lemon juice
1 tablespoon finely chopped onion

Dash pepper
Dash chopped fresh parsley
¼ teaspoon dry mustard
⅛ teaspoon chopped garlic

1. Combine all ingredients in a container with a tight-fitting lid and mix well.
2. Chill and serve over salad.

Serves 4

Per serving: 6.7 calories, 0.3 grams protein, 1.5 grams carbohydrate, 0.02 grams fat.

FRENCH DRESSING

2 tablespoons freshly squeezed lemon juice
2 tablespoons wine vinegar
½ teaspoon paprika
½ teaspoon dry mustard
⅛ teaspoon pepper
⅛ teaspoon tarragon
1 tablespoon salad oil
¾ cup water

1. Combine all ingredients in container with tight-fitting lid and shake well.
3. Chill before serving on salad.

Serves 8

Per serving: 15 calories, 0 grams protein, 0 grams carbohydrate, 1.7 grams fat.

RUSSIAN SALAD DRESSING

¾ cup cider vinegar
¾ cup water
2 tablespoons lemon juice
1 tablespoon chopped onion
1 tablespoon dry mustard
1 teaspoon garlic powder
⅛ teaspoon pepper
½ teaspoon paprika

1. Combine all ingredients and mix well.
2. Shake before each use.

Serves 10

Per serving: 0.4 calories, 0.01 grams protein, .09 grams carbohydrate, 0 grams fat.

WINE-APPLE DRESSING

2 ounces wine vinegar
1 ounce water
1 teaspoon undiluted frozen apple juice concentrate,
    thawed
Dash pepper

1. Combine all ingredients and mix well
2. Pour over salad

Serves 1

Per serving: 2.4 calories, 0 grams protein, 0.6 grams carbohydrate, 0 grams fat.

GARDEN DRESSING

½ cup vegetable oil
¼ cup vinegar
¼ cup sliced onion
¼ cup chopped fresh parsley

1 tablespoon finely chopped green pepper
¼ teaspoon snipped fresh chives
¼ teaspoon dried basil
1 teaspoon dry mustard
⅛ teaspoon pepper

1. Shake all ingredients together in tightly covered container.
2. Cool overnight.
3. Shake before using.

Serves 8

Per serving: 122 calories, 0 grams protein, 0.4 grams carbohydrate, 14 grams fat.

FRUITY DIP

2 cups low-fat dry-curd cottage cheese
⅔ cup skim milk
2 teaspoons snipped fresh chives
2 teaspoons lemon juice
½ cup mandarin orange segments
5 strawberries
½ cup fresh pineapple cubes
1 peach, pitted and sliced
5 seedless grapes

1. Place all ingredients in blender and blend for 1 minute on low and 1 minute on high.
2. Refrigerate 4 hours or more before serving. (You may use this as a dip with carrots or celery, etc.)

Makes 8, ⅓-cup servings

Per serving: 84.2 calories, 8.8 grams protein, 9.6 grams carbohydrate, 2 grams fat.

VEGETABLE DIP

1 cup low-fat cottage cheese
3 tablespoons skim milk
2 tablespoons chopped green pepper
1 tablespoon chopped green onion
¼ teaspoon chopped fresh parsley
¼ teaspoon dried chives
1 teaspoon chopped fresh spinach

1. Place all ingredients in blender and blend on low speed for 1 minute. Blend on medium speed for another ½ minute.
2. Chill for 2 hours before serving.

Serves 2

Per serving: 112.5 calories, 16 grams protein, 5.7 grams carbohydrate, 2 grams fat.

9
POULTRY AND DAIRY DISHES

Chicken: the bodybuilder's staff of life. The skinned white meat of chicken has come to be known as the sustaining food of the contest-minded bodybuilder. But it has also come to be known as the most boring food imaginable. We have changed that with some wonderful and exciting recipes. These recipes are so savory that, when tried on children and nonbodybuilding adults, they were rated "delicious," and second helpings were requested. There is everything from "fruity" to "creamed" chicken here, not to mention Chicken Shish Kebab.

Chicken, turkey, and egg whites provide an excellent source of low-calorie protein. The reason is quite simple: they are among the lowest in fat (beef being the highest in fat and certain fishes the lowest). In this cookbook, we have taken special care to provide you with the most delicate combinations of fruits, vegetables, and seasonings (in small portions) so that your "plain old" chicken or turkey or egg white will no longer be plain—or old. It will be new and exciting.

You may notice that the fat-containing yolk is almost always eliminated from recipes containing eggs. A little cooking trick to help you adapt other recipes is to substitute two egg whites for every egg yolk.

Whether you are looking for an exciting breakfast (First-Place Fluffy Omelette), an interesting lunch (Szechuan Chicken Crunch) or an unusual dinner (Blasted Chicken), you can refer to this chapter and be sure that you will be neither bored nor disappointed.

POULTRY

Chicken

FABULOUS FRUITY CHICKEN

½ chicken breast (8 ounces), skinned and boned
1 tablespoon grated onion
¼ teaspoon tarragon
⅛ teaspoon pepper
¼ cup orange juice
1 banana, sliced into chunks
5 grapes, halved and seeded (use a dark grape)

1. Cut chicken into ½-inch chunks and place in a non-stick skillet.
2. Add onion, tarragon, pepper, and orange juice.
3. Cook over moderate heat, stirring constantly, until chicken turns white. Then add bananas and grapes.
4. Simmer, covered, over low heat for 5 minutes. (Add more orange juice, if necessary.)

Serves 1

Per serving: 382 calories, 38 grams protein, 46.6 grams carbohydrate, 9.8 grams fat.

BLASTED CHICKEN

4 (8-ounce) chicken breast halves, skinned
Vegetable oil
2 tablespoons red wine
Dash pepper
Dash oregano
Dash onion powder
2 tomatoes, diced
½ cup chopped onion
½ cup chopped green pepper
2 cloves garlic, crushed
1 tablespoon tarragon

1. Brown chicken breasts in a nonstick skillet after coating the bottom with oil by wiping with a paper towel soaked in oil.
2. Over medium heat, add wine, pepper, oregano, and onion powder to chicken.
3. Lower to simmer and add tomatoes, onion, green pepper, and crushed garlic and cook for 5 minutes.
4. Add tarragon and cover and simmer for 5 more minutes.
5. When chicken is done, serve.

Serves 2

Per serving: 260 calories, 39.6 grams protein, 11 grams carbohydrate, 9.3 grams fat.

CREAMED CHICKEN

4 chicken breasts, skinned
2 tablespoons spicy mustard
1 cup water
½ cup white wine
⅛ teaspoon marjoram
¼ teaspoon dried basil
⅛ teaspoon oregano
½ cup plain low-fat yogurt
2 tablespoons unbleached flour
Parsley, for garnish

1. Place chicken in large nonstick skillet.
2. Mix mustard with water, white wine, and seasonings and pour over chicken. Cover and bring to a boil.
3. Uncover and simmer for 20 minutes.
4. Mix yogurt with flour and stir into chicken.
5. Cover and simmer for 10 minutes.
6. Garnish with parsley and serve hot or cold with white rice.

Serves 4

Per serving: 254.2 calories, 39.5 grams protein, 5.9 grams carbohydrate, 9.8 grams fat.

Converted rice, per ¾-cup serving: 167 calories, 3 grams protein, 37 grams carbohydrate, 0.3 grams fat.

CHAMPION CHICKEN STEW

2 pounds chicken, skinned
1 onion, sliced thin
2 large sprigs fresh dill
1 sprig fresh parsley
2 tomatoes, peeled and diced
4 carrots, scraped and cut into chunks
4 potatoes, peeled and quartered
4 celery stalks, cut into chunks
1 cup dry white wine
2 tablespoons lemon juice
1 bay leaf
¼ teaspoon pepper

1. Place chicken in Dutch oven and add onion, dill, and parsley.
2. Arrange tomatoes, carrots, potatoes, and celery around the chicken and add wine, lemon juice, bay leaf, and pepper.
3. Cover and bake in a 350°F oven for 1½ hours.
4. Chill and skim excess fat.
5. Reheat and serve.

Serves 4

Per serving: 438 calories, 43 grams protein, 45 grams carbohydrate, 9 grams fat.

ROUND II HULA CHICKEN

4 8-ounce chicken breasts, skinned
1 large onion, sliced thin
1½ cups juice from pineapple packed in its own juices
½ teaspoon garlic powder
1 teaspoon chopped fresh parsley
½ teaspoon ground ginger
2 green peppers, diced
1 cup uncooked converted rice

1. Place chicken, onion, pineapple juice, seasonings, and

green pepper in a large nonstick skillet.
2. Add uncooked rice and cook, covered, for 25 minutes over a low flame.

Serves 4

Per serving: 299 calories, 13 grams protein, 56 grams carbohydrate, 2 grams fat.

BROILED CHICKEN BREASTS A L'ORANGE

1 8-ounce chicken breast, skinned
2 tablespoons undiluted frozen orange juice concentrate, thawed
⅛ teaspoon tarragon
⅛ teaspoon dried parsley flakes
⅛ teaspoon dry mustard

1. Arrange chicken in broiler pan.
2. Combine orange juice concentrate, tarragon, parsley, and mustard. Mix well and brush half over chicken.
3. Broil for 7 minutes or until chicken is slightly browned.
4. Turn and brush other side with remaining liquid mixture and broil about 12 minutes, until chicken is done.

Serves 1

Per serving: 207 calories, 30 grams protein, 3.6 grams carbohydrate, 11 grams fat.

CHICKEN SHISH KEBAB

6 small tomatoes
¼ cup minced onion
¼ cup minced parsley
¼ cup lemon juice
1 tablespoon low-sodium soy sauce
2 cloves garlic, minced
1 teaspoon coriander seed
2 pounds boned, skinned chicken breasts

1. Combine tomatoes, onion, parsley, lemon juice, soy
   sauce, garlic, and coriander seed in blender and blend
   on low speed until smooth.
2. Cut chicken into 1-inch cubes.
3. Thread chicken onto 4 or 8 skewers.
4. Cook for 20 minutes in a broiler or over an open fire,
   continually basting with sauce.

Serves 4

**Per serving: 252 calories, 39 grams protein, 11 grams
carbohydrate, 9 grams fat.**

PITA CHICKEN

1 8-ounce chicken breast, boned, skinned, broiled, and
   diced
1 medium tomato, diced
1 tablespoon minced green pepper
Dash pepper
⅛ teaspoon onion powder
⅛ teaspoon oregano
1 whole wheat pita round

1. Place chicken, tomato, green pepper, and seasonings
   in bowl and mix well.
2. Fill pita with mixture and serve.

Serves 1

**Per serving: 370 calories, 44 grams protein, 31 grams
carbohydrate, 9 grams fat.**

SZECHUAN CHICKEN CRUNCH

1 large orange
2 8-ounce chicken breasts, boned and skinned
½ cup orange juice
1 tablespoon low-sodium soy sauce
1 tablespoon sherry
1 tablespoon cornstarch
¼ teaspoon crushed red pepper
¼ teaspoon ginger
1 tablespoon vegetable oil
1 cup sliced green onion
½ cup sliced water chestnuts

1. Peel orange and cut rind into thin strips.
2. Place peel in nonstick baking dish and bake for 30 minutes in a 300°F oven. Remove and save.
3. Cut chicken into 1½-inch pieces.
4. Combine orange juice, soy sauce, sherry, cornstarch, red pepper, and ginger and blend well. Set aside.
5. Add oil to 6-quart electric wok and preheat for 2 minutes to 325°F. Add chicken and stir-fry for 3 minutes.
6. Add onions and water chestnuts. Stir-fry 1 minute.
7. Stir in sauce. Let cool 1 minute and add in rest of ingredients.
8. Sprinkle with orange peel before serving.

Serves 4

Per serving: 205 calories, 20 grams protein, 17 grams carbohydrate, 8 grams fat.

HEARTY RUSSIAN CHICKEN SOUP

1 3-pound chicken, skinned and cut into serving-size
  pieces
3 stalks celery, sliced into 1-inch pieces
3 onions, peeled
3 carrots, cut into thirds
1 parsnip, peeled
2 sprigs fresh parsley
¼ teaspoon pepper

1. Place chicken in 4-quart pot and fill pot with water.
2. Bring to a boil and skim water of fat.
3. Place celery, onions, carrots, parsnip, parsley, and
   pepper in water.
4. Simmer for 1 hour.
5. Cool and skim fat. (To get all the fat off, refrigerate
   and then skim.)
6. Reheat and serve.

Serves 8

**Per serving: 198 calories, 24 grams protein, 11 grams
carbohydrate, 8 grams fat.**

BAKED CHICKEN A LA ORANGE

1 3-pound broiler chicken, skinned and cut into serving-
  size pieces
3 tablespoons grated orange peel
½ cup orange juice
¼ teaspoon pepper
1 teaspoon dry mustard
1 teaspoon paprika
¼ teaspoon red pepper sauce
1 4-ounce can mushrooms
1 tablespoon vegetable oil

1. Wash and dry chicken and place in nonstick baking
   pan.
2. Mix remaining ingredients and pour over chicken.

3. Bake, uncovered, for 40 minutes in a 400°F oven.
4. Turn chicken and recoat with sauce on bottom of pan.
5. Bake, uncovered, for 10 minutes or until done.

Serves 4

Per serving: 305 calories, 45 grams protein, 4 grams carbohydrate, 15 grams fat.

GORILLA CHICKEN GUMBO SOUP

1 16-ounce can okra, drained
¼ cup chopped onion
¼ cup chopped green pepper
4 cups chicken broth
1 16-ounce can low-sodium tomatoes
½ teaspoon pepper
1 cup diced cooked chicken
1 bay leaf
1 tablespoon chopped fresh parsley
3 cups cooked converted rice

1. Place okra, onion, and green pepper in nonstick pan.
2. Cook on low heat until onion is soft.
3. Stir in chicken broth, tomatoes, pepper, chicken, bay leaf, and parsley.
4. Simmer, uncovered, for 20 minutes.
5. Serve with ¾ cup rice per bowl.

Serves 4

Per serving: 285 calories, 15 grams protein, 54 grams carbohydrate, 2 grams fat.

OFF-SEASON CHICKEN

4 pounds frying chicken pieces, skinned
2 teaspoons garlic powder
⅛ teaspoon pepper
8 dried figs, halved
1 apple, cored and sliced into rings
½ cup dried apricots
¼ cup raisins
1 cup water
1 cup dry white wine
⅛ cup natural honey
2 teaspoons hot dry mustard
½ teaspoon rosemary

1. Sprinkle chicken with garlic powder and pepper.
2. Bake in a 350°F oven for 45 minutes in a medium nonstick pan.
3. Combine figs, apple, apricots, raisins, water, wine, honey, mustard, and rosemary.
4. Boil fruit mixture for 30 minutes.
5. Remove chicken and pour fruit mixture over chicken.
6. Use a baster to lift juices from baking pan and spread over chicken and fruit. Bake in 400°F oven for 15 minutes.
7. Serve over rice. (Rice not included in calculations.)

Serves 4

Per serving: 603 calories, 62 grams protein, 56 grams carbohydrate, 23 grams fat.

THE CRANE'S GINGER CHICKEN

1 onion, cut into thin strips
¼ cup water
5 cloves garlic, chopped
Oil
1 2-pound broiler chicken, skinned and cut into 2-inch
    pieces
2 tablespoons low-sodium soy sauce
2 tablespoons gingerroot, chopped fine
2 tablespoons fresh mint leaves
8 dried Chinese mushrooms, soaked in hot water, stems
    removed, and sliced
5 green onions, cut into 1-inch pieces
1 teaspoon dried red pepper flakes
2 tablespoons Chinese rice vinegar
2 cups cooked rice
1 tablespoon vegetable oil

1. Heat onions in ¼ cup water in a nonstick pan. When
   onions are limp, add garlic and heat for 2 minutes.
   Remove from heat.
2. Coat a wok with oil and stir-fry chicken in wok for 2
   minutes.
3. Add soy sauce, gingerroot, and mint leaves. Mix and
   add mushrooms, green onions, and red pepper flakes.
   Mix. Add onion and garlic mixture.
4. Cook and stir until chicken is cooked.
5. Add rice vinegar and rice and remove from heat.
6. Serve hot.

Serves 4

**Per serving: 394 calories, 41 grams protein, 37 grams
carbohydrate, 12 grams fat.**

CHICKEN PARMESAN

¼ cup Italian bread crumbs
¼ cup grated Parmesan cheese
⅛ teaspoon garlic powder
⅛ teaspoon oregano
⅛ teaspoon dried basil
4 8-ounce chicken breasts, skinned
½ cup skim milk
2 egg whites, whipped with fork, beaten lightly

1. Mix bread crumbs and Parmesan cheese with garlic powder, oregano, and basil.
2. Dip chicken in mixture of milk and egg whites, then in bread crumb mixture.
3. Repeat dipping in milk and egg white mixture and bread crumbs.
4. Place chicken in shallow pan and broil on each side for 12 minutes or until done.

Serves 4

Per serving: 242 calories, 23 grams protein, 26.3 grams carbohydrate, 10 grams fat.

CHICKEN SOUP

4 chicken breasts, skinned, boned
4 quarts cold water
6 large carrots, halved
5 large onions, halved
2 celery stalks, halved
½ teaspoon pepper
1 teaspoon thyme
1 bay leaf
1 teaspoon chopped fresh parsley
6 peppercorns

1. Place chicken in 8-quart pot.
2. Add water, carrots, onions, celery, pepper, thyme, bay leaf, and parsley. Cover and bring to a boil.

3. Reduce heat and simmer for 2 hours, adding pepper-corns after 1 hour of cooking.
4. Let soup cool and remove fat from top.
5. Reheat and serve.

Serves 4

Per serving: 330 calories, 40 grams protein, 30 grams carbohydrate, 9 grams fat.

COQ AU VIN

4 8-ounce chicken breasts, skinned
1 cup white wine
8 small white onions, sliced
2 cloves garlic, minced
¼ cup tomato paste
2 teaspoons thyme
2 teaspoons dried basil
2 cups sliced mushrooms
1 teaspoon pepper
1 cup water

1. Place skinned chicken in a 4-quart pot.
2. Add wine, onions, garlic, tomato paste, thyme, basil, mushrooms, pepper, and water.
3. Cook, covered, 1½ hours over medium heat.
4. Uncover and add water, if necessary. If too thin, let cook another half hour.
5. Serve hot.

Serves 4

Per serving: 322 calories, 40 grams protein, 18 grams carbohydrate, 9 grams fat.

Turkey
LEVEL III TURKEY ROAST

1 cup white wine
½ teaspoon garlic powder
⅛ teaspoon pepper
⅛ teaspoon sage
⅛ teaspoon thyme
1 2-pound white meat turkey roast
2 tablespoons flour
¼ cup water

1. Mix wine, garlic powder, pepper, sage, and thyme.
2. Bake turkey as directed on turkey wrapper, basting with wine mixture every 15 minutes.
3. Remove roast and cover with foil when done.
4. Remove broth and drippings from pan and skim fat, saving liquid.
5. Mix flour and water in a separate bowl.
6. Heat broth and drippings in a pot and add flour-water mixture, stirring constantly until gravy thickens. Boil and stir 1 minute. Serve gravy with sliced turkey.

Serves 4

Turkey, per serving: 430 calories, 71 grams protein, 0 grams carbohydrate, 13 grams fat.

Gravy, per 1-tablespoon serving: 53 calories, 0 grams protein, 5 grams carbohydrate, 2 grams fat.

DAIRY DISHES
SCRAMBLED EGGS AND VEGGIES

8 egg whites
3 tablespoons minced onions
¾ teaspoon garlic powder
3 tablespoons water
Vegetable oil
1 cup diced tomatoes
1 cup boiled and diced potatoes
1 cup diced zucchini

1. Beat egg whites, onion, garlic powder, and water until mixture is slightly frothy.
2. Wipe bottom of a nonstick skillet with a paper towel soaked in vegetable oil.
3. Cook and stir tomatoes, potatoes, and zucchini for 2 minutes in frying pan.
4. Pour egg mixture over vegetables.
5. As mixture begins to set at bottom and sides of the pan, gently lift cooked portions with spatula so that the uncooked portions can flow to the bottom of the pan.
5. Continue this process until eggs are thick and cooked but still moist.

Serves 2

Per serving: 169 calories, 16 grams protein, 23 grams carbohydrate, 0.4 grams fat.

OVER-EASY ONION JUMPING JACKS

1 onion, sliced
Water
4 egg whites
2 tablespoons grated cheese
½ teaspoon dried dill
Dash pepper

1. Simmer onions in a little water in a nonstick pan until onions are tender.
2. Beat egg whites until soft peaks form.
3. Add cooked onions to egg whites along with grated cheese and dill.
4. Pour mixture into nonstick skillet and cook over low heat until browned.
5. Flip jumping jack and cook other side until lightly browned and firm.

Serves 2

Per serving: 67 calories, 3 grams protein, 8 grams carbohydrate, 1 gram fat.

FIRST-PLACE FLUFFY OMELETTE

1 egg white
1 tablespoon chopped onion
1 teaspoon minced green pepper
1 teaspoon grated cheese

1. Beat egg white until soft peaks form.
2. Add onion, green pepper, and grated cheese.
3. Pour egg mixture into small heated nonstick skillet until underside is lightly browned.
4. Turn and cover.
5. Cook until other side is lightly browned.

Serves 1

Per serving: 24 calories, 3 grams protein, 0.3 grams carbohydrate, 0.5 grams fat.

UNIVERSAL LOW-FAT RICOTTA CHEESE

½ gallon skim milk
½ cup fresh lemon juice

1. Scald milk and remove from heat.
2. Stir lemon juice into milk.
3. Let sit for 15 minutes.
4. Strain to remove liquid.
5. Press curds to remove as much liquid as possible.
6. Refrigerate.

Serves 4

Per serving: 172 calories, 16 grams protein, 23 grams carbohydrate, 0 grams fat.

10

FISH
DISHES

"Which food, as a bodybuilder, do you hate the most?" I asked a former Mr. America and Mr. Universe. "Fish," he immediately replied. "Why?" I asked. "Tuna and flounder, tuna and flounder, tuna and flounder. After a while you get sick of it," he said.

Fish has always been the most sought-after source of protein for the bodybuilder. The reason is simple: It provides the greatest amount of protein for the lowest price in calories, especially flounder, sole, and tuna.

But what do you do about all that boredom? You follow the recipes provided here. How can anyone be bored with Chilled Swordfish with Rosemary or Broiled King Crab Legs?

We include in this chapter recipes for preparing not only sole, tuna, and flounder, but also shrimp, crab, snapper, swordfish, cod, halibut, whitefish, and salmon. The lowest in sodium are flounder and sole. When using tuna (canned in water, of course) be sure to rinse the tuna twice to eliminate most of the sodium used to preserve the tuna. This is especially important if you are five or fewer days away from a contest date.

FISH

Cod

FISH CAKES

1 pound cod fillets
1 bay leaf
2 cups finely chopped onion
3½ cups mashed potatoes
½ cup chopped fresh parsley
2 teaspoons Worcestershire sauce
¼ teaspoon pepper
Pinch ground cloves
4 egg whites
1 tablespoon vegetable oil
2 cups whole wheat bread crumbs
1 cup whole wheat flour

1. Place fish fillets in pot and cover with water, adding bay leaf and onions. Simmer for 25 minutes, drain, and discard seasonings.
2. Place fish, potatoes, ¼ cup parsley, Worcestershire sauce, pepper, and cloves in large bowl and blend with electric mixer. Shape into 12 cakes.
3. Beat egg whites with oil until frothy.
4. Combine bread crumbs and remaining parsley.
5. Coat fish cakes with flour.
6. Dip fish cakes in egg mixture and coat with bread crumbs.
7. Fry fish cakes for 7 minutes on each side in a non-stick frying pan.

Serves 4

Per serving: 517 calories, 35 grams protein, 75 grams carbohydrate, 7.1 grams fat.

Flounder
BAKED FLOUNDER WITH VEGETABLES

2 pounds flounder fillets
¼ teaspoon pepper
1 onion, grated
1 green pepper, diced
6 medium tomatoes, sliced thin
1 bay leaf
1 carrot, scraped and sliced thin
½ lemon, sliced thin

1. Arrange fillets in a flat nonstick baking dish and sprinkle with pepper.
2. Spread onion and green pepper around flounder fillets.
3. Spread tomatoes over fillets.
4. Add bay leaf and carrot slices.
5. Arrange thin slices of lemon over fillets.
6. Bake in a 350°F oven for 25 minutes.

Serves 4

Per serving: 253 calories, 41 grams protein, 17 grams carbohydrate, 3.3 grams fat.

SPINACH STUFFED FLOUNDER

4 6-ounce flounder fillets
1 10-ounce package frozen chopped spinach, thawed
¼ cup scallions, sliced thin
¼ teaspoon ground nutmeg
⅛ teaspoon paprika
¼ cup white wine
2 tablespoons chopped fresh dill

1. Spread flounder slices flat.
2. Combine thawed spinach, scallions, and nutmeg.
3. Spread spinach mixture in a thin layer over each fillet.
4. Roll up fillets and fasten each with a toothpick.
5. Place fillets in nonstick baking dish.
6. Sprinkle fish with paprika and pour white wine and lemon juice around fish.
7. Sprinkle chopped dill over everything and bake in a 350°F oven for 25 minutes.

Serves 4

Per serving: 167 calories, 31 grams protein, 4 grams carbohydrate, 2.2 grams fat.

BAKED SUPERMAN'S FLOUNDER

1½ pounds flounder fillets
Paprika to taste
Dash dried basil
Dash dried bell peppers
Dash oregano
Dash crushed red pepper flakes
2 tomatoes, sliced
8 ounces low-fat mozzarella cheese, cut into chunks

1. Sprinkle both sides of fish with paprika, basil, bell peppers, oregano, and red pepper flakes.
2. Place fish in shallow baking dish and cover with sliced tomatoes.
3. Place mozzarella chunks on top of tomato slices.

4. Sprinkle once again with all seasonings.
5. Bake in a 375°F oven for 15 minutes.
6. You will know the fish is ready when the cheese is melted.

Serves 4

Per serving: 309 calories, 45 grams protein, 5.2 grams carbohydrate, 11.7 grams fat.

Halibut
MONTE CARLO "GOOD MORNINGS"

1½ pounds halibut steaks, 1 inch thick
¼ teaspoon pepper
⅛ teaspoon garlic powder
⅛ teaspoon paprika
¼ cup orange juice
1 tablespoon lemon juice
1 teaspoon dried chervil leaves
Lemon wedges

1. Sprinkle fish with pepper, garlic powder, and paprika.
2. Mix orange juice with lemon juice and chervil.
3. Cover fish and broil for 20 minutes, periodically brushing with orange juice mixture.
4. Cut into serving-size pieces and serve.

Serves 4

Per serving: 182 calories, 36 grams protein, 1.7 grams carbohydrate, 2 grams fat.

Salmon
BAKED SALMON WITH LEMON

4 8-ounce salmon steaks
¼ cup lemon juice
2 teaspoons marjoram
2 teaspoons onion powder
½ teaspoon pepper
½ teaspoon paprika

1. Heat oven to 425°F and place fish in nonstick baking pan.
2. Mix lemon juice, marjoram, onion powder, pepper, and paprika and spoon over fish.
3. Bake for 30 minutes.

Serves 4

Per serving: 492 calories, 51 grams protein, 0 grams carbohydrate, 30.4 grams fat.

POACHED DILL SALMON

1 quart water
1 tablespoon vinegar
¼ teaspoon tarragon
Dash pepper
2 8-ounce salmon fillets
Fresh dill sprigs

1. Combine water and vinegar with tarragon and pepper in nonstick frying pan.
2. Bring to a boil over medium heat.
3. Reduce heat to low and add salmon.
4. Cover and poach 6 minutes.
5. Add fresh dill sprigs to taste.

Serves 2

Per serving: 492 calories, 51 grams protein, 0 grams carbohydrate, 30.4 grams fat.

SALMON SALAD WITH ARTICHOKES

1½ pounds cooked salmon
Salmon Dressing (recipe follows)
1 head romaine lettuce
1 pound asparagus, cooked
1 pound new potatoes, cooked and cut into chunks
1 cup sliced carrots
2 tomatoes, cut into wedges
1 6-ounce jar artichoke hearts, halved
2 tablespoons grated Romano cheese

1. Break cooked salmon into large chunks and set aside.
2. Make Salmon Dressing (recipe follows) and set aside.
3. Line platter with romaine lettuce leaves.
4. Place salmon in center and surround with asparagus, potatoes, carrots, tomatoes, and artichoke hearts.
5. Top with Romano cheese and dressing.

Serves 4

Per serving: 566 calories, 47 grams protein, 41 grams carbohydrate, 24 grams fat.

SALMON DRESSING

3 tablespoons olive oil
½ cup Dijon mustard
2 cloves garlic, crushed
3 tablespoons lemon juice
¼ teaspoon dried basil
1½ tablespoons chopped fresh parsley
1 tablespoon capers
Dash pepper

1. Combine all ingredients in a tightly covered container and shake well.
2. Chill and serve or serve as is over Salmon Salad with Artichokes.

Serves 4

Per serving: 95 calories, 0.1 grams protein, 0.4 grams carbohydrate, 10.5 grams fat.

Snapper
BAKED SNAPPER

1 large onion, chopped
2 stalks celery, chopped
½ pound mushrooms, sliced
1½ pounds red snapper
2 tablespoons lemon juice
1 teaspoon Worcestershire sauce

1. Place onion, celery, and mushrooms on bottom of nonstick baking pan and place fish on top.
2. Mix lemon juice and Worcestershire sauce and pour over fish.
3. Bake, uncovered, in a 350°F oven for 20 minutes.

Serves 4

Per serving: 177.6 calories, 31 grams protein, 8.7 grams carbohydrate, 2.2 grams fat.

Sole
BAKED FILLET OF SOLE

1 large onion, chopped
1 carrot, chopped fine
1½ pounds sole fillets
Dash pepper
½ cup dry white wine
½ cup water
2 tablespoons lemon juice
¼ cup chopped fresh parsley

1. Place onion and carrot on the bottom of a nonstick baking dish and arrange fish over mixture.
2. Season with pepper and add wine and water. Cover with foil.
3. Bake for 20 minutes in a 350°F oven.
4. Remove fish to a plate and strain juices into a pot.
5. Cook juices for 10 minutes over a low flame. Add

lemon juice and parsley and cook 1 minute more.
6. Pour lemon mixture over fish and serve.

Serves 4

Per serving: 184 calories, 29.3 grams protein, 6.7 grams carbohydrate, 2.1 grams fat.

BROILED SOLE VERONIQUE

¼ cup lemon juice
1 8-ounce slice fillet of sole
1 tablespoon low-fat yogurt
⅛ teaspoon paprika
Dash onion powder
8 seedless grapes

1. Pour lemon juice over fish and let stand in the refrigerator, covered with aluminum foil, for 30 minutes.
2. Spread fish with yogurt and sprinkle with paprika and onion powder. Place in nonstick baking dish and arrange grapes around fish.
3. Broil for 10 minutes or until done.

Serves 1

Per serving: 188 calories, 39.4 grams protein, 10.6 grams carbohydrate, 3.5 grams fat.

SOLE SEVICHE

1 pound broiled sole fillets, cut into ½-inch cubes
Juice of 6 lemons
Juice of 2 oranges
½ cup dry white wine
½ small onion, chopped fine

1. Place all ingredients in a bowl and mix well.
2. Cover and refrigerate overnight.
3. Remove juice and serve.

Serves 2

Per serving: 327 calories, 41 grams protein, 29.6 grams carbohydrate, 3.4 grams fat.

EASY CHEESY PINWHEEL APPETIZERS

1 pound sole fillets
¼ cup grated Parmesan cheese
½ teaspoon dry parsley flakes
¼ teaspoon lemon pepper seasoning
⅛ teaspoon garlic powder
¼ cup lemon juice
Dash paprika
Dash oregano

1. Wash and dry sole and cut into 3-inch strips, ½ inch wide.
2. Mix cheese, parsley, lemon pepper, and garlic powder.
3. Coat fish with cheese mixture and roll into small circles. Fasten with a toothpick.
4. Place circles in shallow nonstick baking pan and brush with lemon juice.
5. Sprinkle with paprika and oregano and bake in a 425°F oven for 15 minutes.
6. Serve hot or cold.

Serves 4

Per serving: 112.5 calories, 41 grams protein, 0.1 grams carbohydrate, 2.8 grams fat.

BAKED FILLET OF SOLE WITH ASPARAGUS

1 8-ounce fillet of sole
6 cooked asparagus spears
⅓ cup water
3 tablespoons chopped fresh tomatoes
1 tablespoon finely chopped onion
1 tablespoon white wine
¼ teaspoon thyme
Dash pepper
Chopped fresh parsley to taste

1. Fold fish around asparagus spears and pin with toothpick.
2. Combine water, tomatoes, onions, wine, thyme, and pepper in baking dish and place fish in mixture. Cover with foil.
3. Bake 15 minutes in a 350°F oven.
4. Pour juices over fish and sprinkle with parsley.

Serves 1

Per serving: 230 calories, 42 grams protein, 9 grams carbohydrate, 3 grams fat.

Swordfish

CHILLED SWORDFISH WITH ROSEMARY

1 tablespoon oil
2 large onions, cut into rings
3 tablespoons water
10 ounces swordfish, cubed
1 bay leaf
¼ cup red wine vinegar
½ teaspoon white pepper
⅛ teaspoon rosemary
Onion powder to taste
Chopped parsley to taste

1. Heat oil in nonstick frying pan and saute onions over medium heat until onions are soft.
2. Add water and fish and saute for 4 minutes more.
3. Add bay leaf, vinegar, pepper, rosemary, and onion powder and saute for 1 minute more.
4. Remove from heat and refrigerate for at least 5 hours. Add parsley and serve.

Serves 2

Per serving: 275.1 calories, 29.1 grams protein, 11 grams carbohydrate, 9 grams fat.

Tuna

TUNA TRADE-OFF

1 10-ounce package frozen green beans
1 7-ounce can water-packed tuna, drained
⅛ teaspoon oregano
1 teaspoon dried sweet bell peppers
⅛ teaspoon thyme
⅛ teaspoon dried basil
3 tablespoons lemon juice
Dash pepper
Dash garlic powder
3 tablespoons white wine

1. Place frozen green beans on a 24-inch sheet of foil.
2. Top green beans with tuna.
3. Make dressing by combining remaining ingredients and pour over fish.
4. Seal in foil, place in baking dish, and bake at 400°F for 20 minutes.

Serves 2

Per serving: 168 calories, 29 grams protein, 5.7 grams carbohydrate, 1 gram fat.

CHILLED TUNA AND RICE WITH TOMATOES

1 7-ounce can water-packed tuna, drained and rinsed
3 cups cooked enriched rice
⅓ cup chopped scallions
2 teaspoons curry powder
3 teaspoons lemon juice
3 tablespoons wine vinegar
1 teaspoon garlic powder
⅛ cup water
Lettuce leaves
1 tomato, sliced

1. Flake tuna and add to rice.
2. Add scallions, curry powder, lemon juice, vinegar, and garlic powder to mixture.
3. Add ⅛ cup water.
4. Place mixture in bowl and refrigerate for 3–5 hours or overnight.
5. Arrange on lettuce leaves with sliced tomato.

Serves 4

Per serving: 242 calories, 17.6 grams protein, 39.4 grams carbohydrate, 0.7 grams fat.

TUNA FRUIT SALAD

1 pear, chopped
1 slice pineapple, chopped
1 7-ounce can water-packed tuna, flaked and drained
½ cup low-fat yogurt
½ teaspoon curry powder
½ teaspoon vanilla
¼ cup raisins
1 apple, chopped
Lettuce leaves

1. Mix all ingredients except lettuce, tossing until well combined.
2. Line a large plate with lettuce leaves.
3. Arrange mixture on lettuce leaves and serve chilled.

Serves 2

Per serving: 345 calories, 33 grams protein, 51 grams carbohydrate, 2.8 grams fat.

Whitefish

WHITEFISH ROUNDS WITH DILL

2 onions
1 carrot, scraped
2 sprigs fresh parsley
1 sprig fresh dill
2 cups water
2 pounds whitefish fillets
2 egg whites
⅛ cup unbleached flour
½ teaspoon white pepper

1. Place 1 onion, carrot, parsley, and dill in pot with water and bring to a boil. Then reduce heat to simmer.
2. Grind fish and the remaining onion in blender.
3. Beat egg whites until frothy, adding them to fish and beating again for 1 minute in blender.

4. Add flour and pepper and blend for 1 minute. Transfer from blender to bowl.
5. Form into fish balls and place in simmering liquid. Cover and simmer for 1 hour.
6. Remove fish balls with slotted spoon and serve hot or cold.

Serves 4

Per serving: 399 calories, 45.7 grams protein, 8.8 grams carbohydrate, 18.7 grams fat.

SHELLFISH

Crab

BROILED KING CRAB LEGS

12 ounces Alaskan king crab legs, split and thawed
1 tablespoon lemon juice
2 teaspoons grated onion
1 clove garlic, crushed
1 tablespoon chopped fresh parsley
¼ teaspoon tarragon
Dash hot red pepper sauce

1. Remove crabmeat from shells and cut into small pieces.
2. Combine remaining ingredients and return crabmeat to shells.
3. Brush mixture over crab legs.
4. Broil crab legs for 4 minutes, brushing with sauce every minute.

Serves 4

Per serving: 80.5 calories, 14.7 grams protein, 1 gram carbohydrate, 1.6 grams fat.

CRAB AND AVOCADO SALAD

8 ounces frozen crabmeat, thawed
½ cup sliced celery
⅓ cup diced green pepper
⅓ cup sliced water chestnuts
1 14-ounce can pineapple chunks in natural juices
¼ cup slivered toasted almonds
2 teaspoons lemon juice
½ teaspoon curry powder
Lettuce leaves
1 avocado, peeled and sliced

1. Drain and slice crabmeat.
2. Combine remaining ingredients except lettuce and avocado, and mix with crab in a bowl.
3. Arrange crab mixture on lettuce leaves.
4. Add avocado slices to top of crab mixture.

Serves 4

Per serving: 267 calories, 13 grams protein, 29 grams carbohydrate, 12.4 grams fat.

Shrimp

CASHEW SHRIMP CURLS

1½ tablespoons cornstarch
¼ teaspoon baking soda
⅛ teaspoon pepper
1 pound shrimp, shelled and deveined
1½ cups water
1 cup rice
1 tablespoon margarine
¾ cup water
1 cup chopped onion
1 clove garlic, minced
1 teaspoon minced gingerroot
1 cup cubed zucchini
½ cup diced red pepper
½ cup unsalted cashew nuts

1. Combine cornstarch, baking soda, and pepper in large bowl.

2. Halve shrimp lengthwise and add to bowl.
3. Toss shrimp until well coated and let stand at room temperature for 15 minutes.
4. Bring 1½ cups water to a boil in a medium pot and add rice and margarine. Simmer, covered, for 20 minutes and remove from heat. Let stand 5 minutes.
5. Cook shrimp in nonstick skillet with ¾ cup water until shrimp are pink. Remove shrimp from skillet and set aside.
6. Saute onion, garlic, and gingerroot in shrimp water in nonstick skillet. When onions are limp, add zucchini and red pepper.
7. Cook for 2 minutes more and stir in cooked rice, shrimp, and cashews.
8. Toss until well heated and serve.

Serves 4

Per serving: 324.7 calories, 26 grams protein, 29 grams carbohydrate, 12 grams fat.

WORLD-CLASS SHERRY SHRIMP

2 green onions, chopped
½ cup white wine
¼ teaspoon garlic powder
½ cup sherry
Juice from 1 lemon
1 pound cooked, peeled, deveined shrimp
1 cup sliced fresh mushrooms
⅛ cup grated Parmesan cheese

1. Simmer onions in white wine in a nonstick skillet.
2. Season with garlic powder.
3. Add sherry, lemon juice, shrimp, and mushrooms.
4. Sprinkle mixture with Parmesan cheese.
5. Simmer over low heat until shrimp are cooked.
6. Serve in bowls in juice or over white rice.

Serves 4

Per serving: 194 calories, 22.6 grams protein, 9.2 grams carbohydrate, 1.7 grams fat.

CANTONESE SHRIMP AND SNOW PEAS

¼ cup green onion, sliced thin
1 clove garlic, crushed
1½ pounds cooked, peeled, deveined shrimp
1 teaspoon salad oil
1 teaspoon ground ginger
Dash pepper
1 6-ounce package frozen Chinese snow peas
1½ cups chicken broth
1½ tablespoons cornstarch
½ cup boiling water
Dash thyme

1. Cook onion, garlic, and shrimp in oil in a skillet for 3 minutes, stirring often.
2. Stir in ginger, pepper, snow peas, and chicken broth.
3. Cover and simmer 7 minutes.
4. Dissolve cornstarch in water.
5. Add cornstarch to shrimp and cook until thick and clear, stirring constantly.
6. Sprinkle with thyme and serve.

Serves 4

Per serving: 209 calories, 33 grams protein, 11 grams carbohydrate, 2.6 grams fat.

CHILLED SHRIMP AND CORN SALAD

½ pound small shrimp
2 cups frozen corn kernels
Water
1 cup chopped celery
Curry powder to taste
Pepper to taste
Oregano to taste

1. Rinse shrimp with cold water and dry with paper towels.
2. Refrigerate shrimp.

3. Boil corn in 3 inches of water until tender. Drain and rinse with cold water.
4. Combine all remaining ingredients and add to shrimp and corn. Refrigerate for 1 hour and serve.

Serves 2

Per serving: 232 calories, 25 grams protein, 32 grams carbohydrate, 1.7 grams fat.

Tom Platz.

11

MEAT DISHES

Beef has always been a controversial source of protein for bodybuilders because of its high fat content. Some beef products have as much as 97 percent fat.

Over the years, bodybuilders have gone back and forth on the beef issue, advocating lots of beef in the '50s and '60s, shunning it altogether in the 1970s, and now apparently feeling that some people can handle it while others cannot. The reality is that some bodybuilders actually need beef in order to keep up muscle size. They seem to be able to use and burn the fat without having it "stick." In fact they seem to need the fat contained in beef in order to maintain size. Other bodybuilders, however, consider beef taboo, especially anywhere from 12 to 8 weeks before contest time. They find that eating beef makes them fat, and they avoid it completely.

The recipes in this chapter are provided for those people who can eat beef, but they are carefully designed to eliminate all excess calories. Only the leanest cuts are called for, and as much fat as possible is trimmed before cooking. By taking careful note of the fat grams, you will be able to ensure that you do not exceed your fat limit.

Beef
LEAN 'N' MEAN SHISH KEBAB

4 ounces lean sirloin tip steak, cut into 1-inch squares,
   trim fat
4 cherry tomatoes
½ green pepper, cut into 1-inch cubes
4 mushroom caps
1 8-ounce can boiled white onions
1 teaspoon cider vinegar
¼ cup freshly squeezed tomato juice
¼ teaspoon dry mustard
⅛ teaspoon garlic powder
Dash pepper

1. Thread meat, tomatoes, green pepper, mushroom
   caps, and onions alternately onto shish kebab
   skewers.
2. Heat vinegar, tomato juice, mustard, garlic powder,
   and pepper in a small pot.
3. Place skewers in broiler about 3 inches away from
   heat and brush tomato juice mixture on meat and
   vegetables. Broil for 7 minutes, turning and brushing
   with mixture every 1½ minutes.

Serves 1

**Per serving: 427 calories, 22.2 grams protein, 21.5 grams
carbohydrate, 28.4 grams fat.**

HEAVYWEIGHT RED-WINE ROUND STEAKS

4 6-ounce round steaks, beaten and thinned
1 cup dry red wine
1 clove garlic, crushed
⅛ teaspoon oregano
⅛ teaspoon dried basil
Pepper to taste

1. Place steaks on foil in broiler pan.

2. Pour wine over steaks.
3. Rub garlic into steaks on both sides.
4. Add oregano and basil to both sides of steak.
5. Sprinkle with pepper to taste.
6. Broil to taste.

Serves 4

Per serving: 375.6 calories, 33.2 grams protein, 2.6 grams carbohydrate, 20 grams fat.

PERSONAL BEST BEEFSTEAK AND POTATOES

1 pound round steak (1 inch thick), trim fat
2 tablespoons flour
⅛ cup water
3 onions, sliced thin
¼ teaspoon pepper
⅛ teaspoon thyme
⅛ teaspoon garlic powder
2 cups water
3 potatoes, peeled and sliced thin
¼ teaspoon paprika

1. Cut meat into 1-inch cubes and coat with flour (shake off and reserve excess flour).
2. Brown meat in a nonstick skillet and drain fat.
3. Add ⅛ cup water and onions and cook until onions are soft.
4. Pour mixture into pot and sprinkle with remaining flour, pepper, thyme, and garlic powder.
5. Pour 2 cups water over mixture, cover, and bake in a 350°F oven for 45 minutes.
6. Arrange potatoes on meat and increase oven temperature to 450°F. Bake, uncovered, for 25 minutes.

Serves 4

Per serving: 338 calories, 26 grams protein, 27 grams carbohydrate, 13.7 grams fat.

SUPERSTAR SIRLOIN TIP

1 6-ounce piece sirloin tip
¼ cup dry burgundy
¼ teaspoon onion powder
2 large mushrooms (caps intact, stems chopped fine)
¼ teaspoon dried dill
Dash pepper
Dash garlic powder
1 medium tomato
¼ teaspoon chopped fresh parsley
1 teaspoon Italian bread crumbs

1. Soak beef in wine for 15 minutes, turning beef 3 times.
2. Remove beef from wine, reserving wine. Sprinkle beef with onion powder and place on broiler pan.
3. Mix chopped mushroom stems with dill, pepper, and garlic powder and stuff mushroom caps with the mixture.
4. Place mushroom caps on broiler pan next to steak.
5. Cut tomato in half and sprinkle with parsley and bread crumbs. Place in broiler pan next to steak.
6. Pour remaining burgundy over meat, mushrooms, and tomatoes.
7. Broil for 3–5 minutes. Turn steak and broil for another 3–5 minutes.

Serves 1

Per serving: 588 calories, 28 grams protein, 11 grams carbohydrate, 42 grams fat.

STEAK SALAD OLYMPIA

1½ pounds sirloin steak
1 4-ounce jar sliced mushrooms, drained and rinsed
1 medium green pepper, sliced into rings
⅓ cup red wine vinegar
¼ teaspoon garlic powder
½ teaspoon onion powder
¼ teaspoon pepper
¼ teaspoon tarragon
2 cloves garlic, crushed
8 lettuce leaves
4 cherry tomatoes

1. Broil steak for 10 minutes on each side or to taste and cut into ½-inch strips. (Save juices for marinade.)
2. Arrange beef strips on a plate and place mushrooms and pepper rings on top of meat.
3. Combine vinegar and seasonings and pour over meat and vegetables.
4. Refrigerate overnight, covered, spooning beef cooking juices as a marinade over mixture from time to time.
5. Make lettuce cups using 2 large lettuce leaves.
6. Place meat mixture on lettuce and add cherry tomatoes.
7. Serve cold.

Serves 4

Per serving: 516 calories, 28 grams protein, 4.2 grams carbohydrate, 42.1 grams fat.

BIG-TIME BEEF BURGUNDY

5 medium onions, sliced
½ pound mushrooms, stemmed and sliced
2 pounds lean round steak, cut into 1-inch cubes
¼ teaspoon marjoram
¼ teaspoon thyme
⅛ teaspoon pepper
1½ teaspoons unbleached flour
½ cup water
1¾ cups burgundy

1. Cook onions and mushrooms in a nonstick skillet until both are soft.
2. Remove from pan, add meat and ¼ cup water.
3. Sprinkle with marjoram, thyme, and pepper.
4. Mix flour and water and ½ cup wine and stir into pan.
5. Heat to a boil, stirring constantly, and cook for 1 minute.
6. Add the rest of the wine and cover and cook for 1½ hours over a low flame.
7. Add more water and wine (1 part water to 2 parts wine) if necessary.
8. Stir in onions and mushrooms and cook for 10 minutes.

Serves 4

Per serving: 588 calories, 48 grams protein, 18 grams carbohydrate, 27 grams fat.

AMIGO ARTICHOKE BURGER BLASTS

4 medium artichokes
1 pound lean ground round
Dash pepper
¼ teaspoon oregano
¼ teaspoon basil
2 slices whole wheat bread
Water

¼ cup finely chopped carrots
1 tomato, chopped fine

1. Trim bases of artichokes, pull off small tough leaves around bottoms, and trim off top ½ inch or so of leaves with scissors. Core artichokes by spreading leaves from center and scooping out the choke (fuzzy inside part).
2. Combine ground round, pepper, oregano, and basil, and mix well in a bowl.
3. Soak bread in water and squeeze out water.
4. Add bread to meat mixture and mix well.
5. Stuff artichokes.
6. Bake in a 350°F oven for 20 minutes.

Serves 4

Per serving: 288 calories, 28 grams protein, 18 grams carbohydrate, 12 grams fat.

MONSTER MUSHROOM MOUSSAKA

1½ pounds lean ground beef
2 onions, diced
1 cup sliced mushrooms
1 6-ounce can low-sodium tomato paste
1 cup water
¾ cup dry white wine
2 tablespoons chopped fresh parsley
⅓ teaspoon ground cinnamon
½ teaspoon ground nutmeg
⅛ teaspoon pepper
⅓ cup whole wheat bread crumbs
1 eggplant, peeled and sliced thin
Dash ground nutmeg

1. Brown meat in a nonstick skillet and drain fat.
2. Add onions, mushrooms, tomato paste, water, wine, parsley, cinnamon, ½ teaspoon nutmeg, and pepper. Cover and simmer for 40 minutes.
3. Stir in bread crumbs. Remove mixture to medium-sized nonstick baking dish and add layer of eggplant slices. Continue to layer meat mixture with eggplant until used up.
4. Sprinkle with additional nutmeg and bake in a 350°F oven for 45 minutes.

Serves 4

Per serving: 443 calories, 39 grams protein, 23 grams carbohydrate, 18 grams fat.

BEEF MANICOTTI

6 whole wheat manicotti pasta shells
1 pound lean ground beef
1 tablespoon chopped onion
¼ teaspoon ground nutmeg
1 cup low-sodium farmer cheese
¼ cup skim milk
2 teaspoons chopped fresh parsley
1 egg white
2 cups juice from low-sodium tomatoes
¼ cup low-sodium tomato paste
⅓ teaspoon garlic powder
½ teaspoon oregano
¼ teaspoon dried basil

1. Boil manicotti shells until still slightly hard.
2. Mix beef, onions, and nutmeg and fry in a nonstick pan until meat and fat separate. Drain fat.
3. Mix cheese with skim milk and parsley and add to meat mixture.
4. Beat egg white until frothy and add to meat mixture.
5. Combine tomato juice, tomato paste, garlic powder, oregano, and basil. Cover and cook until mixture boils. Lower heat.
6. Stuff meat mixture into manicotti shells and bake in a tomato sauce-lined baking dish at 325°F for 30 minutes, basting with extra sauce from time to time.

Serves 4

Per serving: 500 calories, 44 grams protein, 50 grams carbohydrate, 13 grams fat.

BAKED STUFFED PEPPERS

2 large green peppers
1 cup water
½ pound lean ground beef
1 cup dry whole wheat bread crumbs
1 tablespoon chopped onion
¼ teaspoon oregano
¼ teaspoon dried basil
¼ teaspoon pepper
1 8-ounce can low-sodium tomato sauce

1. Cut tops off green peppers and remove seeds and pith. Wash.
2. Heat water and bring to boil.
3. Stand peppers upright in water and cook 5 minutes. Drain water.
4. Mix remaining ingredients and stuff peppers with them.
5. Stand peppers upright in nonstick baking pan and bake, covered, in a 325°F oven for 45 minutes.
6. Uncover and bake for 5 minutes. Serve.

Serves 2

Per serving: 469 calories, 38 grams protein, 71 grams carbohydrate, 15 grams fat.

PRECONTEST HAMBURGER PICKUP

6 ounces very lean ground round
2 mushrooms, sliced thin
1 slice raw onion
Water
⅛ teaspoon dry mustard
Dash red pepper
Dash garlic powder
1 tablespoon whole wheat flour

1. Place ground beef in bowl.

2. Simmer mushrooms and onion in ½ inch water in nonstick pan.
3. Cook until mushrooms are tender and pour mixture into bowl of ground beef. Add mustard, red pepper, garlic powder, and flour and mix well.
4. Form a patty and broil to taste.

Serves 1

Per serving: 342 calories, 36.4 grams protein, 8 grams carbohydrate, 17 grams fat.

CHECKLIST CHILI

1 pound lean ground beef
1 large onion, chopped
2 pounds canned kidney beans, rinsed twice
1 pound canned crushed low-sodium tomatoes
2 tablespoons chili powder
Dash pepper
Dash onion powder

1. Brown beef and onion in a large nonstick skillet and drain all fat.
2. Add remaining ingredients and mix.
3. Cover and simmer for 1 hour.

Serves 4

Per serving: 446 calories, 36 grams protein, 45.2 grams carbohydrate, 12.5 grams fat.

MEAT LOAF AMERICA

1 pound lean ground beef
2 tablespoons chopped onion
1 clove garlic, crushed
½ cup oatmeal
4 egg whites
¼ teaspoon oregano
¼ teaspoon rosemary
¼ teaspoon chopped fresh parsley
½ cup juice from freshly squeezed tomatoes

1. Mix all ingredients together in a bowl.
2. Pat into a medium nonstick baking pan.
3. Bake in a 350°F oven for 30 minutes.
4. Drain all fat and serve sliced.

Serves 4

Per serving: 245 calories, 27.7 grams protein, 5 grams carbohydrate, 11.6 grams fat.

TOTAL BODY BEEF PIZZA

1 pound lean ground beef
1 teaspoon garlic powder
½ cup skim milk
½ cup whole wheat bread crumbs
1 8-ounce can low-sodium tomato sauce
1 cup sliced mushrooms
4 ounces skim-milk mozzarella cheese, sliced
1 teaspoon oregano
2 tablespoons grated Parmesan cheese

1. Mix beef, garlic powder, milk, and bread crumbs together in a bowl.
2. Spread over the bottom of a medium nonstick baking pan.
3. Spread tomato sauce on top of meat mixture and add mushrooms.

4. Top with mozzarella cheese and sprinkle with seasonings and Parmesan cheese.
5. Bake in a 400°F oven for 30 minutes.
6. Drain all fat and let stand for 5 minutes.
7. Cut into slices and serve.

Serves 4

**Per serving: 375 calories, 39 grams protein, 27 grams
carbohydrate, 18 grams fat.**

BIG BILL'S SLOPPY GYMS

1 pound ground sirloin tip
1 16-ounce can Ragu cooking sauce
¼ teaspoon oregano
¼ teaspoon basil
¼ teaspoon thyme
Dash hot red pepper
Dash black pepper
⅛ teaspoon chili powder
4 whole wheat pita rounds

1. Brown meat in a skillet and drain all fat.
2. Pour Ragu cooking sauce onto meat and simmer for 5
   minutes with oregano, basil, thyme, hot pepper, black
   pepper, and chili powder.
3. Spoon into whole wheat pita rounds and serve.

Serves 4

**Per serving: 263 calories, 28.4 grams protein, 21 grams
carbohydrate, 11.8 grams fat.**

SPORTS BEEF AND VEGETABLES

1 pound lean ground beef
4 potatoes, cut into ¼-inch slices
2 large carrots, cut into ¼-inch slices
1 large onion, cut into ¼-inch slices
1 16-ounce can low-sodium tomatoes, cubed
1 green pepper, cut into ¼-inch slices
Dash pepper
Dash dried basil
Dash garlic powder

1. Brown hamburger meat in a nonstick skillet and drain all fat.
2. Top meat with layers of potatoes, carrots, onion, tomatoes, and green pepper.
3. Season with pepper, basil, and garlic powder.
4. Cover and simmer for 30 minutes.

Serves 4

Per serving: 380 calories, 29 grams protein, 39.1 grams carbohydrate, 12 grams fat.

Lamb

LIGHTWEIGHT LAMB SHISH KEBAB

1 teaspoon lemon juice
1 pound leg of lamb, cubed
Dash pepper
1 onion, sliced
3 tomatoes, cut into wedges
1 bay leaf
2 green peppers, cut into 1-inch squares
6 eggplant slices, cut into 1-inch squares

1. Rub lemon juice onto meat.
2. Sprinkle meat with pepper.
3. Place meat on a flat plate and cover with onion, tomatoes, and bay leaf. Refrigerate overnight.

4. Arrange meat on skewers, alternating with onion squares, eggplant squares, tomato wedges, and green pepper squares.
5. Barbecue or broil.

Serves 4

Per serving: 266 calories, 19.5 grams protein, 12 grams carbohydrate, 15.8 grams fat.

LAMBURGERS

1 pound ground lamb
2 slices protein bread
1 small onion, chopped
⅛ teaspoon pepper
⅛ teaspoon oregano
⅛ teaspoon dried basil
⅛ teaspoon garlic powder
1 egg white
Sliced tomato and onion for garnish

1. Mix ground lamb with all other ingredients except garnish. Blend well.
2. Shape into patties and fry in a nonstick skillet until done, turning once.
3. Place on paper towels to drain excess fat.
4. Serve with sliced tomato and onion.

Serves 4

Per serving: 318 calories, 18.6 grams protein, 5 grams carbohydrate, 24 grams fat.

Veal

VICTORY VEAL CHOPS AND VEGETABLES

4 medium 8-ounce veal chops
1 clove garlic, crushed
¼ teaspoon thyme
¼ teaspoon pepper
1 onion, sliced
1 carrot, diced
1 stalk celery, sliced thin
¾ cup dry red wine
1 tablespoon tomato paste
1 tablespoon lemon juice
1 teaspoon wine vinegar
1 cup water
4 medium potatoes, peeled

1. Coat chops with garlic, thyme, and pepper.
2. Mix onion, carrot, and celery together and place on the bottom of a nonstick baking dish that is big enough to hold chops in one layer.
3. Place chops over mixture.
4. Mix wine, tomato paste, lemon juice, and vinegar with water.
5. Pour over chops and place potatoes around chops.
6. Bake in a 350°F oven for 30 minutes.

Serves 4

Per serving: 539 calories, 37 grams protein, 33 grams carbohydrate, 24.7 grams fat.

VEAL STEW WITH ROSEMARY

4 thick veal cutlets (8 ounces each), cut into 3-inch cubes
2 onions, diced
1 clove garlic, crushed
1 bay leaf
1 teaspoon rosemary
¾ cup dry white wine
1 carrot, grated
1 celery stalk, chopped fine
¼ cup chopped fresh parsley
2 cups cubed fresh tomatoes
⅓ cup water

1. Brown veal cubes in nonstick skillet.
2. Add onions, garlic, bay leaf, rosemary, and white wine. Cover and simmer for 4 minutes.
3. Add carrot, celery, parsley, and tomatoes and stir in water. Mix well.
4. Cover and simmer for 25 minutes and serve with ¼ cup white rice per serving. (Rice is not included in calculations.)

Serves 4

Per serving: 436 calories, 38.6 grams protein, 14 grams carbohydrate, 21 grams fat.

LUCKY AND LEAN VEAL PARMESAN

1 pound veal round steak
½ cup Italian bread crumbs
¼ cup grated Parmesan cheese
⅛ teaspoon pepper
⅛ teaspoon paprika
2 egg whites
3 tablespoons water
1 8-ounce can low-sodium tomato sauce
½ teaspoon oregano
¼ teaspoon dried basil

1. Cut meat into 4 pieces.
2. Pound into ¼-inch thick pieces.
3. Mix bread crumbs with cheese, pepper, and paprika.
4. Beat eggs until slightly frothy.
5. Dip meat into egg, then into bread crumb mixture.
6. Brown meat on both sides in a nonstick skillet.
7. Add water and cover and simmer for 30 minutes. Remove from heat.
8. Pour tomato sauce mixed with oregano and basil into a pot and boil.
9. Pour sauce over meat and serve.

Serves 4

Per serving: 286 calories, 24 grams protein, 24.5 grams carbohydrate, 15 grams fat.

MARTINI VEAL CHOPS

1 teaspoon olive oil
4 lean 8-ounce veal chops
Pepper to taste
6 tablespoons gin
2 tablespoons dry vermouth
Thyme to taste
Chopped fresh parsley to taste

1. Heat olive oil in a nonstick skillet and saute veal chops

in it for 10 minutes. Sprinkle chops with pepper on both sides and remove from pan. Wipe pan to remove excess oil.
2. Add gin, vermouth, thyme, and pepper to pan.
3. Simmer mixture until half is evaporated, then add parsley, pour over chops, and serve.

Serves 2

Per serving: 500 calories, 33 grams protein, 6 grams carbohydrate, 27 grams fat.

VEAL CHOPS MOZZARELLA

2 8-ounce veal chops
2 ounces low-fat mozzarella cheese, thinly sliced
¼ cup whole wheat flour
Pinch pepper
2 egg whites, slightly beaten
2 cups whole wheat bread crumbs
Low-sodium tomato juice
Dash white pepper
Dash dry parsley flakes

1. Cut a pocket in each chop by cutting to the bone.
2. Pound chops until they are ½ inch thick, then place cheese in the pockets and secure with a toothpick.
3. Combine flour and pepper and coat chops.
4. Dip chops into egg whites and then bread crumbs. Repeat.
5. Saute chops in ½ inch of tomato juice for 7 minutes on each side.
6. Season with pepper and parsley and serve.

Serves 2

Per serving: 922 calories, 59 grams protein, 90 grams carbohydrate, 34 grams fat.

BROILED VEAL CHOP WITH TOMATO AND HERBS

1 8-ounce veal rib chop
1 small tomato
½ small onion, diced
½ green pepper, diced
⅛ teaspoon rosemary
⅛ teaspoon tarragon
⅛ teaspoon dried basil
Water

1. Place veal chop on broiling pan and broil for 6 minutes on each side or until done.
2. Cut tomato into small pieces and place in a nonstick skillet with onion, green pepper, rosemary, tarragon, and basil.
3. Cook over low heat until onion is tender, adding a small amount of water when necessary.
4. Serve chops with onion mixture on top of them.

Serves 1

Per serving: 413 calories, 35 grams protein, 11 grams carbohydrate, 25 grams fat.

12

RICE, POTATO, PASTA, AND GRAIN DISHES

For years people have thought that any self-respecting dieter would never even dream of eating spaghetti or potatoes. Well, that myth will be dispelled quickly once you see how low in calories and how high in complex carbohydrates these dishes are.

In this section you can delight yourself with Winner's Linguine with Red Clam Sauce, Scalloped Potatoes, Bran Muffins, and yes, even Pizza.

As a bodybuilder, you need to feel as if you have eaten a hearty meal. You need to come away from the table with that satisfied feeling of having eaten something with substance. Oh, salads and vegetables are wonderful, but let's face it—we all need something solid and down to earth once in a while. Here you will find wonderful recipes that are high in complex carbohydrates and low in calories. You may be surprised to find that you can eat, without guilt, some of your favorite rice, potato, bread, and pasta dishes. The secret here is that we have eliminated the cooking demons, such as oils, butter, salt, and cream. Instead, we have provided you with the essential, healthy vegetable and seasoning bases that leave you feeling satisfied and yet not guilty—and, most important, not fat or bloated, both dreaded by serious bodybuilders.

We suggest that you use protein spaghetti, converted rice, and boiled or baked potatoes because they provide the essential foods and palate satisfaction for the lowest number of calories.

Rice
CHILLED FRUIT AND RICE SALAD

1½ cups low-fat cottage cheese
½ cup skim milk
1 cup strawberries, cut into eighths
½ cup peaches, peeled and cut into small cubes
½ cup pineapple, cut into small cubes
1½ cups chilled cooked converted rice

1. Beat cottage cheese in a blender until smooth, then add milk and beat another minute.
2. Remove from blender and place in a bowl.
3. Add fruits and mix with a wooden spoon.
4. Stir in rice and mix again. Serve cool.

Serves 4

Per serving: 214 calories, 15 grams protein, 34 grams carbohydrate, 2.2 grams fat.

ESTHETIC VEGETABLE RICE

1 cup low-fat buttermilk
1 cup sliced celery
½ cup finely chopped onion
1 teaspoon dry mustard
1½ cups cooked, cooled converted rice
½ cup peeled, diced cucumber
4 radishes, sliced
4 hard-boiled egg whites, chopped

1. Combine buttermilk, celery, onion, and mustard.
2. Stir in cooled rice, cucumber, radishes, and egg whites.
3. Chill 1 hour and serve.

Serves 4

Per serving: 141 calories, 7.5 grams protein, 25.4 grams carbohydrate, 0.7 grams fat.

KIDNEY BEANS AND BROWN RICE

½ onion, chopped
1 tablespoon whole wheat flour
2 tablespoons water
1 cup water
1 15-ounce can red kidney beans, rinsed 3 times to
  remove salt
1 tablespoon chopped fresh parsley
¼ teaspoon chili powder
¼ teaspoon minced garlic
⅛ teaspoon pepper
Dash red hot pepper sauce
1 cup brown rice

1. Cook rice according to directions on package.
2. In a nonstick frying pan, fry onions until slightly brown.
3. Mix flour with 2 tablespoons water and blend mixture into fried onions.
4. Cook for 3 minutes and add 1 cup water.
5. Cook until slightly thickened and add beans and seasonings.
6. Add rice and mix well. Serve.

Serves 4

Per serving: 302 calories, 11.4 grams protein, 61 grams carbohydrate, 1.4 grams fat.

BROWN RICE AND VEGETABLES

1 cup raw brown rice
1 cup pineapple juice (from unsweetened canned
    pineapple in its own juice)
1 cup fresh grapefruit juice
½ cup chopped onion
½ cup chopped celery
¼ cup chopped green pepper
1 teaspoon chopped fresh parsley
½ teaspoon chili powder
⅛ teaspoon pepper

1. Place raw brown rice in a nonstick skillet and heat.
2. Add pineapple juice, grapefruit juice, onion, celery, green pepper, parsley, chili powder, and pepper and mix well.
3. Simmer, covered, for 40 minutes or until done.

Serves 4

Per serving: 254 calories, 5 grams protein, 56.7 grams carbohydrate, 1 grams fat.

STUFFED RICE TOMATOES

4 large tomatoes
3 tablespoons water
1 onion, diced
½ green pepper, diced
2 cups cooked rice
1 tablespoon grated Romano or Parmesan cheese

1. Remove pulp of each tomato, leaving shell for stuffing.
2. Chop tomato pulp fine and place in a nonstick pan with 3 tablespoons water.
3. Add onion and green pepper and simmer over low heat, stirring occasionally, until vegetables are soft.
4. Add cooked rice and mix well.

5. Remove from heat and stuff tomato shells with mixture.
6. Top tomatoes with grated cheese and bake in a 350°F oven for 30 minutes.

Serves 4

Per serving: 158 calories, 4.4 grams protein, 33.5 grams carbohydrate, 0.9 grams fat.

Potatoes
SCALLOPED POTATOES

5 large potatoes, peeled and sliced thin
1 onion, sliced thin
¼ teaspoon ground nutmeg
⅛ teaspoon pepper
1 cup evaporated skim milk

1. Layer potatoes and onion in a nonstick baking pan and sprinkle lightly with nutmeg and pepper.
2. Pour evaporated milk over mixture and bake in 350°F oven for 45 minutes or until done.

Serves 4

Per serving: 200 calories, 9 grams protein, 41 grams carbohydrate, 0.4 grams fat.

IFBB SWEET POTATOES

¼ cup orange juice
¼ teaspoon ground ginger
¼ teaspoon ground nutmeg
2½ cups hot mashed sweet potatoes
2 egg whites

1. Add orange juice, ginger, and nutmeg to hot mashed
   sweet potatoes.
2. Beat egg whites until stiff peaks form and fold egg
   whites into sweet potato mixture.
3. Place potatoes in nonstick baking dish and bake in a
   350°F oven for 30 minutes.

Serves 4

**Per serving: 76 calories, 2.6 grams protein, 15.6 grams
carbohydrate, 0.2 grams fat.**

INTERMEDIATE MASHED POTATOES

4 large potatoes
½ cup skim milk
½ teaspoon pepper
⅛ teaspoon oregano
1 teaspoon lemon juice
Dash paprika

1. Bake potatoes in a 350°F oven or potato baker for 1
   hour or until done.
2. Remove skin and place pulp in large bowl. Mash with
   potato masher.
3. Add skim milk, pepper, oregano, and lemon juice and
   mash until semicoarse.
4. Sprinkle paprika over mixture and serve.

Serves 4

**Per serving: 125 calories, 4.2 grams protein, 27 grams
carbohydrate, 0.2 grams fat.**

POTATO DILL

1 potato, peeled and quartered
1 cup water
¼ teaspoon dried dill
Dash pepper

1. Place potato in pot with water, dill, and pepper.
2. Simmer, covered, until potato is cooked (15–20 minutes).
3. Drain and serve.

Serves 1

Per serving: 114 calories, 3.2 grams protein, 25.7 grams carbohydrate, 0.2 grams fat.

POWER POTATOES

2½ cups grated raw potatoes
½ cup grated onion
2 scraped carrots, grated
¼ teaspoon pepper
¼ teaspoon lemon rind
½ cup potato flour
¼ cup skim milk
4 egg whites

1. Combine grated potatoes, onion, and carrots. Add pepper, nutmeg, and lemon rind.
2. Stir in potato flour and skim milk.
3. Beat egg whites until stiff and fold into potato mixture.
4. Pour into a nonstick baking pan and bake in a 350°F oven for 45 minutes.

Serves 4

Per serving: 171 calories, 7.6 grams protein, 34.7 grams carbohydrate, 0.3 grams fat.

BAKED POTATOES WITH COTTAGE CHEESE

4 large baking potatoes
16 ounces low-fat cottage cheese

1. Bake potatoes for 1 hour in a 350°F oven.
2. Cut a cross in center of each potato.
3. Remove center of potatoes and fill with cottage cheese.

Serves 4

Per serving: 215.5 calories, 19 grams protein, 30 grams carbohydrate, 6.7 grams fat.

MASHED POTATOES

3 medium potatoes
Water
1 small onion, chopped fine
2 cloves garlic, minced
1 bay leaf
2 tablespoons rosemary
2 teaspoons chopped fresh parsley
1 cup skim milk, heated
⅛ teaspoon ground mace

1. Peel potatoes and cover with water in a pot. Bring to a boil.
2. Add onion, garlic, bay leaf, rosemary, and parsley and cook for 30 minutes.
3. Add hot milk and mace, beat with electric mixer until smooth, and serve.

Serves 4

Per serving: 114 calories, 5 grams protein, 24 grams carbohydrate, 0.2 grams fat.

BARBECUED POTATO CRISPS

4 medium potatoes
Dash vinegar
Pepper to taste
Onion powder to taste
Paprika to taste
Parsley to taste

1. Slice potatoes into ¼-inch slices and splash both sides with vinegar.
2. Sprinkle both sides with pepper, onion powder, and paprika.
3. Broil on open flame of charcoal broiler until crisp.
4. Turn and sprinkle with parsley before serving.

Serves 4

Per serving: 114 calories, 3.2 grams protein, 25.7 grams carbohydrate, 0.2 grams fat.

TRAINING PARTNER POTATO PANCAKES

2 pounds potatoes, peeled
1 onion
2 egg whites
2 tablespoons unbleached flour
¼ teaspoon pepper

1. Grate potatoes into bowl.
2. Grate onion into same bowl.
3. Beat egg whites lightly with a fork until frothy and stir in potato mixture.
4. Stir in flour and pepper.
5. Drop batter into large nonstick skillet by large spoonfuls.
6. Brown each side over medium flame and serve.

Serves 4

Per serving: 200 calories, 7.2 grams protein, 4.3 grams carbohydrate, 0.3 grams fat.

HASH BROWNS

4 medium potatoes
Water
2 tablespoons finely chopped onion
½ teaspoon garlic powder
⅛ teaspoon black pepper
1 tablespoon vegetable oil
Sliced tomato, vinegar, and parsley for garnish

1. Peel potatoes and cook in 1 inch boiling water for 30 minutes.
2. Drain and cool, then grate and toss with onion, garlic powder, and pepper.
3. Heat oil in a nonstick skillet and place potato mixture in pan, packing tightly, leaving ¾ inch space around the edges.
4. Cook over low heat for 12 minutes or until crust is formed.
5. Cut into quarters and turn, then brown the other side.
6. Serve with sliced tomato and vinegar. Sprinkle with parsley.

Serves 4

Per serving: 148 calories, 3.3 grams protein, 26.6 grams carbohydrate, 3.7 grams fat.

GRILLED POTATOES WITH LEMON

4 large potatoes, peeled and cubed
Water
1 teaspoon grated lemon peel
¼ cup lemon juice
¼ teaspoon ground nutmeg
¼ teaspoon black pepper
¼ teaspoon garlic powder
¼ teaspoon dry mustard
1 green onion (with top), chopped

1. Cook potato cubes in 1 inch of boiling water until tender.

2. Drain, add remaining ingredients, and mix.
3. Place mixture on large piece of heavy-duty aluminum foil and wrap tightly.
4. Charcoal grill for 30 minutes (15 minutes on each side) or bake in a 350°F oven for 40 minutes.

Serves 4

Per serving: 122 calories, 3.5 grams protein, 27.5 grams carbohydrate, 0.2 grams fat.

POTATO SALAD

2 pounds white potatoes
Water
½ cup finely chopped celery
¼ cup finely chopped green pepper
1 onion, chopped fine
½ cup uncreamed low-fat cottage cheese
⅓ cup skim milk
⅛ teaspoon dry mustard
¼ teaspoon dried dill
¼ teaspoon celery seed
1 teaspoon vinegar
1 teaspoon lemon juice

1. Boil potatoes in water to cover until tender and remove skin while still hot.
2. Cut potatoes into cubes and place in bowl.
3. Add celery, green pepper, and onion and toss.
4. Beat cottage cheese, milk, mustard, dill, celery seed, vinegar, and lemon juice for 3 minutes.
5. Pour sauce into potatoes and toss.
6. Refrigerate for 2 hours before serving.

Serves 4

Per serving: 215 calories, 9.8 grams protein, 43 grams carbohydrate, 0.8 grams fat.

Pasta
WINNER'S LINGUINE WITH RED CLAM SAUCE

1 15-ounce jar Ronzoni Lite 'n' Natural Marinara Sauce
½ cup frozen clams, chopped
½ green pepper, chopped
1 onion, finely chopped
2 tablespoons chopped garlic
½ teaspoon pepper
Dash hot red crushed pepper
1 8-ounce package high protein linguine
Water

1. Pour sauce into a pot and add clams, green pepper, onion, garlic, pepper, and crushed red pepper.
2. Simmer for 30 minutes on very low flame.
3. Drop linguine into 3 quarts of boiling water and boil until done to taste.
4. Drain linguine and serve with clam sauce poured on top.

Serves 4

Per serving: 278 calories, 21.3 grams protein, 69 grams carbohydrate, 2.2 grams fat.

CHAMPION SPAGHETTI AND WHITE WINE

½ pound thin protein spaghetti
1 large onion, chopped
1 clove garlic, minced
2 tablespoons chopped fresh parsley
1 teaspoon oregano
½ teaspoon dried basil
3 tablespoons water
½ cup dry white wine
4 egg whites, lightly beaten
6 ounces grated Romano cheese

1. Cook spaghetti according to package directions.
2. Simmer onion, garlic, and seasonings in 3 tablespoons water in nonstick pan until onion is soft.
3. Add wine and cooked spaghetti and mix well.
4. Stir in beaten egg whites and grated cheese and let mixture stand for 2 minutes, covered, before serving.

Serves 4

Per serving: 335 calories, 22 grams protein, 42 grams carbohydrate, 4.6 grams fat.

Grains
OATMEAL WITH BANANAS AND CINNAMON

1 cup rolled oats
2 cups boiling water
½ banana, sliced
⅓ cup skim milk
Dash ground cinnamon

1. Stir oats into boiling water and cook and stir for 5 minutes.
2. Cover oats and let cool for 3 minutes.
3. Add sliced banana and milk, sprinkle with cinnamon, and serve.

Serves 1

Per serving: 224 calories, 8 grams protein, 44 grams carbohydrate, 2.6 grams fat.

WHOLE WHEAT BREAD CRUMBS

10 slices whole wheat bread

1. Leave bread slices on a plate overnight or for at least 5 hours.
2. Grate bread on fine side of potato grater over a large bowl.
3. Place bread crumbs in a plastic container or jar and save at room temperature or refrigerate for future use.

Makes 1 cup

Per 1-tablespoon serving: 34.3 calories, 1.5 grams protein, 6.8 grams carbohydrate, 0.4 grams fat.

WHOLE WHEAT CHEESE AND TOMATO ROUNDS

4 whole wheat English muffins, split
8 tomato slices
4 ounces low-fat mozzarella cheese
¼ teaspoon oregano
¼ teaspoon chopped fresh parsley
½ teaspoon garlic powder

1. Place split English muffins on broiler tray, split sides up.
2. Place 1 slice of tomato on each muffin half.
3. Slice mozzarella cheese into small pieces and place pieces evenly over each English muffin.
4. Sprinkle with oregano, parsley, and garlic powder.
5. Broil for 7 minutes or until cheese is melted.

Serves 4

Per serving: 199 calories, 13 grams protein, 25 grams carbohydrate, 6 grams fat.

BRAN MUFFINS

2 cups whole wheat flour
2 cups unprocessed bran flakes
1½ teaspoons baking soda
2 egg whites
2 cups skim milk
¼ cup undiluted frozen apple juice concentrate, thawed

1. Combine dry ingredients in a bowl.
2. Beat egg whites until stiff peaks form.
3. Add liquid ingredients to dry ingredients and fold in egg whites.
4. Bake in a nonstick muffin tin for 20 minutes in a 400°F oven.

Serves 12

Per serving: 95.5 calories, 3.7 grams protein, 20 grams carbohydrate, 0.3 grams fat.

WILD RICE WITH MUSHROOMS

1 cup raw wild rice
4 cups water
1 pound fresh mushrooms, sliced
½ teaspoon dry white wine
⅛ teaspoon ground nutmeg
⅛ teaspoon pepper

1. Cook wild rice in water according to package directions, not longer than 40 minutes.
2. Place mushrooms, white wine, nutmeg, and pepper in a nonstick skillet and simmer until half the wine has evaporated.
3. Add the mushroom mixture to the rice and place in a nonstick baking pan. Bake at 375°F for 30 minutes or until done.

Serves 4

Per serving: 202 calories, 9 grams protein, 37 grams carbohydrate, 0.6 grams fat.

PIZZA

1 medium onion, chopped
1 green pepper, chopped
1 cup sliced fresh mushrooms
3 tablespoons water
1 6-ounce can low-sodium tomato paste
2 teaspoons oregano
¼ teaspoon garlic powder
⅛ teaspoon hot red pepper
8 slices protein bread, crusts removed
2 tablespoons grated Parmesan cheese
8 ounces skim-milk mozzarella cheese
6 egg whites, beaten
2 cups skim milk

1. Simmer vegetables in water in a nonstick pan until vegetables are tender.
2. Add tomato paste and all seasonings.
3. Place 4 slices of bread in bottom of a nonstick baking dish, spread half the tomato mixture over the bread, and sprinkle with 1 tablespoon Parmesan cheese.
4. Place half the mozzarella over the tomato mixture.
5. Add another layer of bread, tomato, and cheeses.
6. Combine egg whites and milk and pour over bread mixture.
7. Cover and refrigerate overnight or for at least 3 hours, then bake in a 350°F oven for 1 hour and serve.

Serves 4

Per serving: 364 calories, 34 grams protein, 31 grams carbohydrate, 11 grams fat.

13
DESSERT DISHES

Desserts? What place could desserts possibly have in the life of a serious bodybuilder? Well, with a little creativity, a little intelligent planning, there is no reason why a bodybuilder cannot look forward to a treat after dinner just as everyone else does. Yes, even the fat-conscious can enjoy Phantom's Waffles and Strawberries, or Pineapple and Orange Ice Cream Imagination, or even Broiled Fruit Kebabs.

The recipes contained in this section consist of fruits combined with various low-calorie ingredients, giving you another exciting way to consume complex carbohydrates. We also include some wonderful thick shakes and drinks, such as Orange Banana Thick Shake and Onstage Highball. Whether you like baked apples, blueberry pancakes, bread pudding, or raspberry parfaits, you will not be disappointed when you look for your dessert in this chapter.

Our secret lies in eliminating the simple carbohydrates such as sugar and honey and adding fascinating combinations of spices such as nutmeg, cinnamon, and cloves, and the right combinations of yogurts in flavors such as cherry, lemon, strawberry, and banana. Before you know it, you will forget all about the guilt by association connected with dessert and contest shape.

Hot Fruit Desserts
TASK MASTER APPLE PUDDING

1½ cups whole wheat flour
2 cups skim milk
¼ cup undiluted frozen apple juice concentrate, thawed
2 teaspoons vanilla extract
4 egg whites
4 apples, peeled and sliced
¼ cup orange juice
1 teaspoon ground cinnamon
¼ teaspoon ground ginger

1. Combine flour, milk, apple juice concentrate, and vanilla in a bowl.
2. Beat egg whites until foamy, add to flour mixture, and mix well.
3. Peel the apples and spread them in a layer on the bottom of a medium nonstick baking dish.
4. Sprinkle orange juice and then half the cinnamon evenly over the apples. Add the other half of the cinnamon to the batter.
5. Pour the batter over the apples and bake in a 400°F oven for 30 minutes.
6. Cut the pudding into squares and serve.

Serves 4

Per serving: 374 calories, 12.2 grams protein, 78 grams carbohydrate, 1.6 grams fat.

BIG APPLE BEAUTY

1 large apple
Dash ground cinnamon
1 teaspoon undiluted frozen apple juice concentrate, thawed
1 teaspoon raisins
⅛ teaspoon vanilla

1. Core apple and peel skin from top ½ inch of apple.
2. Sprinkle cinnamon into core space and add apple juice concentrate and raisins, which have been dipped in vanilla.
3. Bake in a nonstick baking dish for 30 minutes in a 350°F oven.

Serves 1

Per serving: 125.4 calories, 0.3 grams protein, 28.9 grams carbohydrate, 1 grams fat.

HARD/SOFT APPLE BREAD PUDDING

4 apples, peeled and chopped
6 slices protein bread, cubed
3 cups skim milk
6 egg whites
¼ cup undiluted frozen apple juice concentrate
2 teaspoons ground cinnamon
2 tablespoons cinnamon for topping

1. Place chopped apples and bread cubes in a nonstick baking dish.
2. Combine milk, egg whites, apple juice concentrate, and cinnamon in a bowl and pour over apple mixture.
3. Top with additional cinnamon.
4. Cover and bake in a 325°F oven for 45 minutes.

Serves 4

Per serving: 312 calories, 17 grams protein, 59.3 grams carbohydrate, 1.3 grams fat.

BLUEBERRY AND COTTAGE CHEESE INSANITY

1 cup low-fat cottage cheese
¼ cup skim milk
¾ cup whole wheat flour
2 egg whites
1½ teaspoons lemon juice
1 cup whole fresh blueberries

1. Combine cottage cheese, skim milk, and flour in a bowl.
2. Beat egg whites until frothy but not stiff and add to cottage cheese mixture.
3. Add lemon juice, stir, add blueberries, and stir again.
4. Pour all of the batter into a nonstick frying pan and turn when tops begin to bubble and bottom is lightly browned.
5. Divide into 4 wedges and serve.

Serves 4

Per serving: 154 calories, 11 grams protein, 24 grams carbohydrate, 1.4 grams fat.

PRONE CARROT PUDDING

2 cups scraped and thinly sliced carrots
1 large onion, diced
1 cup skim milk
4 slices whole wheat bread, torn into small pieces
4 egg whites, beaten stiff
1 tablespoon grated orange rind
½ teaspoon ground cinnamon
¼ teaspoon ground allspice
⅛ teaspoon ground nutmeg

1. Steam carrots and onion until tender.
2. Pour skim milk, carrots, onions, orange rind, and spices into blender and blend to a smooth puree.
3. Place bread slices in a bowl and pour puree over

them. Mix lightly and add beaten egg whites.
4. Pour into a nonstick baking dish and bake at 350°F for 45 minutes. The pudding is done when you insert a knife into the middle and the knife comes out clean. The top of the pudding should also be browned.

Serves 4

Per serving: 148 calories, 9 grams protein, 27 grams carbohydrate, 1 grams fat.

BRANDY BANANA PUMPER

1 banana, halved lengthwise
¼ cup unsweetened apple juice
½ teaspoon grated lemon rind
⅛ teaspoon ground ginger
1 tablespoon brandy

1. Arrange banana slices in large skillet.
2. Add apple juice, lemon rind, and ginger and cook over low heat for 6 minutes, basting continually with juice.
3. Heat brandy and pour over bananas.
4. Light the brandy and shake the skillet until the flames go out.
5. Serve immediately.

Serves 1

Per serving: 169 calories, 1.6 grams protein, 41.2 grams carbohydrate, 0.3 grams fat.

BROILED GRAPEFRUIT GRASPS

1 grapefruit
2 tablespoons undiluted frozen apple juice concentrate, thawed
⅛ teaspoon ground cinnamon

1. Cut grapefruit in half and use a grapefruit knife to loosen segments.
2. Spread apple juice concentrate on grapefruit and sprinkle lightly with cinnamon.
3. Broil grapefruit for 7 minutes and serve.

Serves 2

Per serving: 100 calories, 0.6 grams protein, 25.5 grams carbohydrate, 0.1 grams fat.

SHERRY GRAPEFRUIT

2 grapefruit
4 teaspoons sherry

1. Cut grapefruit in half and remove seeds.
2. Loosen sections with grapefruit knife, making room for sherry.
3. Pour 1 teaspoon sherry over each grapefruit half and chill for 1 hour.
4. Broil for 5 minutes and serve hot.

Serves 4

Per serving: 46 calories, 0.5 grams protein, 11 grams carbohydrate, 0.1 grams fat.

ORANGE ENERGY

½ cup natural unsweetened pineapple juice
4 large carrots, sliced thin diagonally
½ cup water

1 pound pineapple chunks (2 cups fresh pineapple chunks)
1 teaspoon cornstarch

1. Place pineapple juice and carrots in saucepan and cook for 10 minutes over low heat. Add ½ cup water and pineapple chunks and cook for 5 minutes.
2. Mix cornstarch with 2 tablespoons pineapple juice and stir into mixture.
3. Cook until thickened and serve.

Serves 4

Per serving: 85 calories, 1.4 grams protein, 21 grams carbohydrate, 0.3 grams fat.

PHANTOM'S WAFFLES AND STRAWBERRIES

1 cup whole wheat flour
1¼ cups skim milk
1 teaspoon vanilla
4 egg whites, beaten stiff
2 cups sliced fresh strawberries
2 tablespoons undiluted frozen apple juice concentrate, thawed
½ teaspoon lemon juice

1. Combine flour, milk, and vanilla, mixing until smooth, and add beaten whites.
2. Pour batter onto a hot nonstick waffle iron and bake until lightly browned.
3. Combine ½ cup sliced strawberries and apple juice concentrate in an electric blender and blend until smooth. Pour over remaining strawberries and use as a topping for the waffles.

Makes 4 waffles

Per serving: 165 calories, 9 grams protein, 30 grams carbohydrate, 0.4 grams fat.

BROILED FRUIT KEBABS

1 cup fresh pineapple chunks
1 orange, peeled and cut into 1-inch squares
15 cherries
1 pear, cut into cubes
4 cooked prunes

1. Alternate fruits on 4 skewers.
2. Place on a nonstick baking pan in broiler or charcoal broil for 2 minutes on each side.

Serves 4

Per serving: 118.7 calories, 1.4 grams protein, 30.3 grams carbohydrate, 0.5 grams fat.

Cold Fruit Desserts
GRAPEFRUIT 'N' YOGURT BOATS

2 small grapefruit
1 7½-ounce can unsweetened mandarin orange segments
1 unpeeled apple, cut into 1½-inch cubes
½ pound seedless grapes
8 ounces low-fat cherry yogurt

1. Cut each grapefruit in half and remove sections by cutting around edges and separating sections with grapefruit knife.
2. Save empty shell.
3. Mix grapefruit sections with orange sections, apple cubes, and grapes and chill.
4. Fill grapefruit shells with mixture and top each with 2 tablespoons yogurt.

Serves 4

Per serving: 189 calories, 4 grams protein, 43 grams carbohydrate, 1.7 grams fat.

MELON STRAWBERRY CHERRY SWEETS

1 cantaloupe
¼ cup strawberries
½ pound fresh cherries
12 watermelon balls
16 seedless grapes

1. Cut a ripe cantaloupe in half and scoop out the seeds. Halve again to make quarters.
2. Arrange strawberries, cherries, melon balls, and grapes on each melon wedge and serve cold.

Serves 4

Per serving: 112 calories, 2.2 grams protein, 27 grams carbohydrate, 0.7 grams fat.

PINEAPPLE BOATS

1 small pineapple
½ pint strawberries
¼ cup undiluted frozen orange juice concentrate, thawed
Pinch ground nutmeg
Pinch ground cinnamon

1. Halve each pineapple lengthwise and save the top. Halve again to make quarters.
2. Cut out inside of pineapple and cut fruit into wedges 1 inch thick.
3. Alternate rows of pineapple pieces and strawberries inside pineapple shells.
4. Sprinkle 1 tablespoon orange juice concentrate, then nutmeg and cinnamon, over each pineapple section.
5. Serve chilled.

Serves 4

Per serving: 134 calories, 1 gram protein, 34.7 grams carbohydrate, 0.4 grams fat.

PINEAPPLE AND CHERRY DELIGHT

1 8-ounce can crushed pineapple (water-packed or in
   own juice)
12 fresh cherries, chopped
1 teaspoon grated orange rind
⅛ teaspoon grated lemon rind

1. Combine pineapple and its liquid and cherries. Divide
   between 2 dessert dishes.
2. Combine grated orange and lemon rinds and top fruit
   with mixture.

Serves 2

**Per serving: 73 calories, 1 gram protein, 18.7 grams
carbohydrate, 0.3 grams fat.**

PINEAPPLE AND ORANGE ICE CREAM
IMAGINATION

1 6-ounce can frozen orange juice concentrate
1 6-ounce can frozen pineapple juice concentrate
3½ cups cold water
2 tablespoons undiluted frozen apple juice concentrate
1 cup nonfat dry milk

1. Put all ingredients into large bowl and beat until
   completely blended.
2. Pour into ice cube trays and freeze until half-frozen (2
   hours).
3. Transfer mixture to mixing bowl and beat with electric mixer on low until soft, then on high for 5 minutes
   until creamy.
4. Pour into freezer molds or ice cube trays and keep
   frozen until ready to serve.

Serves 4

**Per serving: 278 calories, 8 grams protein, 61 grams
carbohydrate, 0.7 grams fat.**

STRAWBERRY AND CANTALOUPE MOVEMENT

2 cantaloupes
1 pint fresh strawberries

1. Cut cantaloupes into halves and remove the seeds.
2. Scallop the edges by making zigzag slices with a knife.
3. Scoop out melon balls with a melon baller.
4. Wash and cut strawberries in half.
5. Mix strawberries and melon balls.
6. Pour mixture into cantaloupe shells and serve.

Serves 4

Per serving: 70 calories, 1.7 grams protein, 17.2 grams carbohydrate, 0.2 grams fat.

FRUIT QUINTETS

2 grapefruit
4 oranges
1 banana, sliced
1 apple, diced
½ cup seedless grapes

1. Remove rind from grapefruit using a grapefruit knife, and discard the rind.
2. Cut oranges in half, remove and discard rind, and slice the sections.
3. Cut grapefruit sections into slices and mix with orange slices, banana slices, diced apple, and seedless grapes.
4. Pour mixture into empty grapefruit shells and serve.

Serves 4

Per serving: 174 calories, 2.5 grams protein, 44 grams carbohydrate, 0.9 grams fat.

RASPBERRY-PINEAPPLE PARFAITS

¼ cup raspberries
½ cup pineapple cut into chunks
8 ounces low-calorie raspberry soda

1. Rinse raspberries and fill parfait glass with alternating layers of raspberries and pineapple chunks.
2. Fill glass with raspberry soda and serve ice-cold.

Serves 1

Per serving: 111 calories, 2 grams protein, 27 grams carbohydrate, 0.7 grams fat.

Thick Shakes and Dessert Drinks
ONSTAGE HIGHBALL

1 quart apple juice
4 cinnamon sticks
12 cloves
1 orange, sliced

1. Combine all ingredients in pot and heat until boiling.
2. Let stand 10 minutes and serve hot.

Serves 4

Per serving: 133 calories, 0.5 grams protein, 33.5 grams carbohydrate, 0 grams fat.

INSPIRATION SPARKLE

1 cinnamon stick
3 cloves
2 tea bags
2 cups water
4 tablespoons undiluted frozen orange juice concentrate
2 cups no-salt seltzer

1. Boil water.

2. Add cinnamon, cloves, tea bags and let stand for 15 minutes.
3. Add orange juice concentrate and pour over ice in tall glasses to one third of glass capacity.
4. Fill the rest of the glass with seltzer.
5. Serve with or without ice cubes.

Serves 4

Per serving: 9.6 calories, 0.1 grams protein, 2.2 grams carbohydrate, 0 grams fat.

ORANGE BANANA THICK SHAKE

1 cup orange juice
1 banana
2 ice cubes
½ cup low-fat yogurt
Dash ground cinnamon

Combine all ingredients in a blender and blend on medium speed until smooth and fluffy.

Serves 1

Per serving: 311 calories, 9.2 grams protein, 59.4 grams carbohydrate, 2.5 grams fat.

MUSCLE MASS BANANA SHAKE

1 cup skim milk
1 banana
1 teaspoon vanilla
2 egg whites
Dash ground cinnamon

Combine all ingredients in a blender, cover, and blend on medium speed until smooth and creamy.

Serves 1

Per serving: 247 calories, 16.3 grams protein, 45.7 grams carbohydrate, 0.7 grams fat.

EGGNOG

1 cup skim milk
¼ cup undiluted frozen orange juice concentrate, thawed
2 egg whites
Dash ground nutmeg
Dash ground cinnamon
3 ice cubes

1. Place all ingredients in blender and blend on high speed, adding the ice cubes one at a time. Blend for 15 seconds on high speed.
2. Serve immediately (before mixture thins out).

Serves 1

Per serving: 151 calories, 15 grams protein, 20 grams carbohydrate, 0.4 grams fat.

PINEAPPLE-LEMON LIFT

1 quart skim milk
1 6-ounce can frozen unsweetened lemonade concentrate
1 1-pound can pineapple chunks

Combine all ingredients in a blender and blend on medium speed until smooth.

Serves 4

Per serving: 167 calories, 9 grams protein, 33 grams carbohydrate, 0.6 grams fat.

BIG BLAST BASIC BLENDER DRINK

1 pint water
2 ounces milk and egg protein mix
6 strawberries or equivalent amount of any other fruit
2 egg whites
4 ice cubes

1. Combine all ingredients in blender on low speed for 10 seconds.
2. Blend on high speed for 1 minute, dropping ice cubes in one at a time.

Serves 2

Per serving: 144 calories, 32.7 grams protein, 2.8 grams carbohydrate, 0 grams fat.

Rachel McLish.

14

CELEBRITY RECIPES AND MEAL PLANS

Here are thirty recipes that were given to us by champion bodybuilders. You will notice that most of them are very low in fat. Some of them are high in carbohydrate, and others are high in protein.

We also include 10 meal plans of the champions. Each of these plans is used by the bodybuilder for approximately three to five days before a contest date.

Most competing bodybuilders go on carbohydrate-loading diets the two days before contest date. This diet has been discussed in previous chapters of this book.

VEGETABLE DISHES

Clarence Bass
(Past 40 Mr. U.S.A.)

STUFFED ACORN COLLARS

2 acorn squash
2 carrots, scraped and grated
1 8-ounce can water-packed crushed pineapple
2 tablespoons white raisins
¼ cup ground ginger

1. Cut squash in half and remove seeds.
2. Place in nonstick baking pan.
3. Combine carrots, pineapple, raisins, and ginger.
4. Place mixture in squash cavities.
5. Bake in a 350°F oven for 30 minutes.

Serves 4

Per serving: 78 calories, 1.6 grams protein, 19.6 grams carbohydrate, 0.2 grams fat.

Lydia Cheng
(Big Apple, Tri-State, East Coast Championships)

CHENG'S LEMON GINGER BROCCOLI

½ 10-ounce package frozen broccoli spears
¼ cup skim milk
1 teaspoon cornstarch
1 teaspoon lemon juice
⅛ teaspoon ground ginger
⅛ teaspoon garlic powder

1. Cook broccoli in 1 inch of water in a small saucepan for 15 minutes.
2. Drain ¼ cup of broccoli water into another pot.
3. Stir milk and cornstarch together, making a thin paste.
4. Stir the paste into the broccoli water.

5. Add lemon juice, ginger, and garlic powder.
6. Bring sauce to a boil, stirring constantly until mixture thickens.
7. Pour sauce over broccoli and serve.

Serves 1

Per serving: 97 calories, 10 grams protein, 18 grams carbohydrate, 0.7 grams fat.

Tim Belknap
(Mr. America)

BELKNAP'S BRUSSELS SPROUT BOMBERS

½ cup cold water
1 10-ounce package frozen Brussels sprouts
½ cup sliced fresh mushrooms
⅛ teaspoon pepper
⅛ teaspoon onion powder
1 tablespoon grated Parmesan cheese

1. Place ½ cup cold water in saucepan and add Brussels sprouts, mushrooms, pepper, and onion powder.
2. Cook until Brussels sprouts are tender.
3. Drain and sprinkle with Parmesan cheese.

Serves 2

Per serving: 53 calories, 5 grams protein, 6 grams carbohydrate, 1 gram fat.

Candy Csencsits
(Ms. Eastern America, 2nd Place Miss Olympia)
CSENCSITS'S STEAMED EGGPLANT

1 medium eggplant
¼ cup lemon juice
¼ teaspoon ground pepper

1. Peel eggplant and halve lengthwise. Halve lengthwise again to make quarters.
2. Brush each piece with lemon juice and sprinkle with pepper.
3. Place in steamer over boiling water and cover tightly.
4. Steam for 20 minutes and serve.

Serves 4

Per serving: 25 calories, 1.2 grams protein, 5.8 grams carbohydrate, 0.2 grams fat.

CHICKEN DISHES AND DAIRY DISHES
Matt Mendenhall
(2nd Place American Championships)
WAIKIKI UNIVERSAL CHICKEN

4 8-ounce chicken breasts, skinned
½ cup unbleached flour
1 tablespoon salad oil
¼ teaspoon pepper
1 4-ounce can sliced pineapple (in its own juices)
½ cup water
¾ cup cider vinegar
¼ teaspoon ground ginger
1 green pepper, cut into ¼-inch rings

1. Wash and dry chicken and coat with flour.
2. In a nonstick skillet, heat oil and brown chicken.
3. Place chicken in shallow roasting pan.
4. Sprinkle with pepper.

5. Make sauce of pineapple juice, water, vinegar, and ginger.
6. Pour over chicken and bake, uncovered, in a 350°F oven for 30 minutes.
7. Add pineapple slices and green pepper rings.
8. Cook for 15 minutes and serve.

Serves 4

Per serving: 291 calories, 39 grams protein, 14 grams carbohydrate, 13 grams fat.

Mike Dayton
(Mr. America)

CHAMPION CHICKEN CHAMPAGNE

2 8-ounce chicken breasts, boned and skinned
1 cup champagne
1 tablespoon finely chopped onion
1 clove garlic, minced
Dash white pepper
2 tablespoons chopped fresh parsley

1. Place chicken breasts between two pieces of waxed paper and pound them thin.
2. Place chicken breasts in nonstick baking pan and add champagne, onion, garlic, and pepper.
3. Bake, covered with Saran wrap, in a 350°F oven for 20 minutes.
4. Remove juices from pan; add parsley, boil for 5 minutes, and pour over chicken. Serve.

Serves 2

Per serving: 309 calories, 37 grams protein, 0.4 grams carbohydrate, 16 grams fat.

Kent Keuhn
(Mr. America; Mr. Universe, Past 40)

CHESTY CHICKEN AND POTATOES

1 8-ounce chicken breast, skinned and cut into bite-sized
pieces
1 potato, cut into ¼-inch slices
Dash pepper
Dash onion powder
Dash paprika
Water
1 10-ounce package frozen string beans

1. Place chicken, potato, and seasonings in a saucepan
   with 1 inch of water.
2. Cover and bring to a boil.
3. Simmer for 20 minutes.
4. Add string beans and cook 5 minutes.
5. Drain and serve.

Serves 1

**Per serving: 324 calories, 41 grams protein, 29 grams
carbohydrate, 9 grams fat.**

Steve Michalik
(Mr. America)

MICHALIK'S OLYMPIC CHICKEN BARBELLS

¼ cup low-sodium soy sauce
1 scallion, chopped
1 teaspoon ground ginger
4 chicken breasts, skinned and boned
12 mushrooms
12 cherry tomatoes
2 green peppers, cut into 1½-inch squares
1 cup rice

1. Mix soy sauce, scallion, and ginger.
2. Cut chicken into cubes.

3. Soak chicken in soy mixture for 30 minutes.
4. Skewer chicken, mushrooms, tomatoes, and green pepper, repeating combination until skewers are filled.
5. Broil over open flame for 5 minutes on each side.
6. Serve with ½ cup cooked rice per serving.

Serves 4

Per serving: 277 calories, 40 grams protein, 17 grams carbohydrate, 9.4 grams fat.
Per 1-cup cooked rice serving: 200 calories, 4 grams protein, 44 grams carbohydrate, 0 grams fat.

Cory and Jeff Everson
(American Mixed Pairs Champions)

EVERSONS' CHICKEN PICCATA

¼ cup whole wheat flour
½ teaspoon pepper
2 8-ounce chicken breasts, boned and skinned
1 clove garlic, chopped
½ teaspoon oil
½ cup dry white wine
2 tablespoons lemon juice
¼ cup chopped fresh parsley

1. Combine flour and pepper and sprinkle over chicken.
2. Brown garlic in oil in nonstick frying pan.
3. Remove garlic and add chicken to pan.
4. Brown chicken 2 minutes on each side.
5. Add wine, lemon juice, and parsley.
6. Simmer 30 minutes.
7. Serve sauce over chicken.

Serves 4

Per serving: 155 calories, 19 grams protein, 6 grams carbohydrate, 5 grams fat.

Dale Ruplinger
(American and World Middleweight Champion)
RUPLINGER'S RIPPED COLD CHICKEN SALAD

4 8-ounce chicken breasts, diced and broiled to taste
1 pound green grapes
2 stalks celery, chopped fine
3 large carrots, chopped fine
¼ teaspoon parsley
¼ teaspoon sage
⅛ teaspoon black pepper
½ fresh lemon
½ pound protein spaghetti

1. Combine cooled chicken, grapes, celery, carrots, parsley, sage, and pepper.
2. Add lemon juice and toss.
3. Cook spaghetti according to package directions. Drain and cool.
4. Place chicken salad in the middle of each of 4 plates and surround with spaghetti.

Serves 4

Per serving: 375 calories, 51 grams protein, 45 grams carbohydrate, 11 grams fat.

David Dupre
(Mr. Pacific Coast, Mr. California)
DUPRE'S WORKOUT CHICKEN AND WHITE WINE SAUCE

4 8-ounce chicken breasts
¼ pound fresh mushrooms, sliced
½ cup dry white wine
1 teaspoon lemon juice
½ teaspoon dried dill
½ cup evaporated skim milk
½ cup Italian bread crumbs

1. Place chicken breasts between two sheets of waxed

paper and pound flat with small mallet.
2. Simmer mushrooms in white wine, lemon juice, and dill until white wine is almost evaporated.
3. Spread mushrooms on flattened chicken breasts, roll them up, and fasten them with toothpicks.
4. Roll breasts in evaporated milk and bread crumbs, completely covering chicken.
5. Arrange chicken in nonstick baking pan and bake in a 350°F oven for 35 minutes or until chicken is tender.

Serves 4

Per serving: 305 calories, 42 grams protein, 15 grams carbohydrate, 10 grams fat.

Laura Combes
(First American Women's Bodybuilding Champion)
CHICKEN POCKETS A TERIYAKI FINALS

1½ pounds chicken, skinned and boned
1 clove garlic, minced
1 tablespoon low-sodium soy sauce
1 tablespoon ground ginger
1 tablespoon sherry
4 large whole wheat pita breads, heated
1 cup shredded lettuce
½ cup finely chopped orange pieces

1. Cut chicken into ½-inch-wide strips (you should have about 20 strips).
2. Combine garlic, soy sauce, ginger, and sherry and pour over chicken.
3. Cover and refrigerate for 1 hour. Drain.
4. Thread chicken strips onto each of 4 skewers and cook for 20 minutes in broiler or on an open flame.
5. Fill each pita bread with chicken from 1 skewer plus shredded lettuce and orange pieces.

Serves 4

Per serving: 251 calories, 25 grams protein, 29 grams carbohydrate, 6.6 grams fat.

Lisa Elliott-Kolakowski
(Gold's Classic Champion)

LISA'S AEROBIC CHICKEN

1 tablespoon vegetable oil
2 scallions, chopped
1 fresh Italian hot pepper
½ cup orange peel, chopped
4 8-ounce chicken breasts, skinned and boned
Dash ground ginger
Dash low-sodium soy sauce
½ cup apple juice
1 cup rice

1. Place oil in nonstick frying pan and brown scallions and hot pepper in it for 5 minutes over a low flame.
2. Add orange peel and fry until peel is brown.
3. Dice chicken and add to frying pan.
4. Sprinkle with ginger.
5. Cook until chicken turns white.
6. Sprinkle with soy sauce.
7. Add apple juice and simmer for 2 minutes.
8. Serve each portion on ½ cup of rice.

Serves 4

Per serving: 317 calories, 39 grams protein, 19 grams carbohydrate, 12.6 grams fat.
Per ½-cup cooked rice serving: 100 calories, 2 grams protein, 22 grams carbohydrate, 0 grams fat.

Tony Emmott
(Mr. World, Mr. Universe)

ORANGE CHICKEN PEC DECS

⅓ cup plain yogurt
1 tablespoon low-sodium, low-fat mayonnaise
4 8-ounce chicken breasts, skinned
¼ cup unbleached flour
2 tablespoons cooking oil

1 medium onion, sliced
Rind from ½ orange, grated
Juice from 1 orange
½ teaspoon crushed tarragon leaves
¼ teaspoon garlic powder
Chopped fresh parsley
2 oranges, peeled, thinly sliced, and halved

1. Combine yogurt and mayonnaise in shallow nonstick baking dish.
2. Dip chicken in mixture and coat with flour.
3. Lightly brown chicken in oil in large nonstick skillet.
4. Add onion, orange peel, and orange juice. Mix.
5. Add tarragon, garlic powder, and parsley to taste. Bring to a boil. Reduce heat to a simmer.
6. Cover and cook over low heat for 30 minutes.
7. Add orange half slices and serve.

Serves 4

Per serving: 374 calories, 40.3 grams protein, 21 grams carbohydrate, 16 grams fat.

Andreas Cahling
(Mr. International)

VEGETARIAN DECLINE BENCH OMELETTE

7 egg whites
1 tomato, chopped
1 cup chopped zucchini
½ green pepper, chopped
Sliced tomato and alfalfa sprouts for garnish

1. Beat egg whites with fork for 1 minute.
2. Add tomato, zucchini, and green pepper.
3. Fry in a nonstick pan, turning when 1 side is brown.
4. Serve with sliced tomato and alfalfa sprouts.

Serves 1

Per serving: 186 calories, 26 grams protein, 17 grams carbohydrate, 0.5 grams fat.

FRUIT

Pat Neve
(Powerlifting World Record Holder)

PAT'S FRUIT SALAD

½ cup fresh strawberries
½ cup fresh sliced peaches
½ cup fresh bing cherries (pitted)
¼ cup fresh red raspberries
2 cups fresh canteloupe balls
¼ cup coarsely chopped walnuts
1 cup plain yogurt
1 teaspoon fructose

1. Mix yogurt and fructose.
2. Fold in fruit and nuts.
3. Chill before serving.

Serves 8

Per serving: 105 calories, 4 grams protein, 20 grams carbohydrate, 1.5 grams fat.

FISH DISHES

Mike Christian
(National and World Champion)

CHRISTIAN'S "BIG BOMBER" WHITE WINE FLOUNDER

1½ pounds flounder fillets
1 large onion, sliced
1 cup dry white wine
7 mushrooms, sliced
Dash pepper
Dash onion powder
Dash paprika
1 tablespoon whole
  wheat flour
½ cup skim milk

1. Place fish in large casserole dish.
2. Add onion, white wine, and mushrooms.
3. Sprinkle with seasonings.
4. Cover and bake in a 350°F oven for 30 minutes.

5. Place fish on a serving platter.
6. Thicken sauce left in pan with flour that has been mixed with cold skim milk.
7. Stir flour and milk mixture into sauce and bring to a boil.
8. Add more pepper, onion powder, and paprika to sauce to taste.
9. Pour sauce over fish and serve.

Serves 4

Per serving: 216 calories, 31 grams protein, 7 grams carbohydrate, 2.1 grams fat.

Richard Gaspari
(Junior Mr. America)
DOUBLE BICEP COD WITH WHITE WINE SAUCE

4 8-ounce codfish steaks
½ cup dry white wine
½ cup chopped onion
½ teaspoon chopped fresh parsley
⅛ teaspoon pepper
⅛ teaspoon paprika
½ lemon, cut into eighths

1. Place codfish steaks in aluminum foil-lined baking dish.
2. Combine white wine, chopped onion, and parsley and pour over fish.
3. Sprinkle both sides of fish with pepper and paprika.
4. Place 2 slices of lemon on each fish.
5. Broil for 10 minutes on each side, or until fish flakes when you break a piece with a fork.

Serves 4

Per serving: 210 calories, 40 grams protein, 3 grams carbohydrate, 1.7 grams fat.

Tom Platz
(Mr. Universe)

PLATZ'S TUNA "BURNS"

1 7-ounce can water-packed tuna
4 ounces raisins
⅓ cup raw wild rice
Water

1. Drain and rinse tuna twice and separate into chunks, lining the bottom of a nonstick baking dish with the chunks.
2. Sprinkle raisins over the tuna.
3. Cover with layer of rice (2 grains thick).
4. Add enough water (about ⅔ cup) to steam.
5. Cover and bake at 275°F for 1 hour.

Serves 1

Per serving: 726 calories, 63 grams protein, 114 grams carbohydrate, 3 grams fat.

Lee Haney
1984 Mr. Olympia

FORCED REPS FISH

1 pound fillet of sole or flounder
Dash garlic powder
½ cup thinly sliced mushrooms
½ cup sherry
2 teaspoons minced onion
1 tablespoon cornstarch
⅓ cup water
2 tablespoons lemon juice
1 tablespoon chopped fresh parsley
7 ounces shrimp, peeled and deveined

1. Split fish into 4 portions and sprinkle with garlic powder.
2. Place mushrooms, sherry, and onions in a nonstick

skillet and cook for 5 minutes over a low flame.
3. Mix cornstarch and water together until smooth and stir into mushroom sauce.
4. Cook, stirring constantly until thick, and stir in lemon juice and parsley.
5. Place each fish portion on a double thickness of foil (about 14 by 10 inches).
6. Place ¼ of the shrimp and ¼ of the mushroom sauce over each fish portion and wrap securely in foil.
7. Cook over coals (about 4 inches from heat) for 20 minutes.

Serves 2

Per serving: 199.4 calories, 28 grams protein, 7.4 grams carbohydrate, 1.7 grams fat.

Charles Glass
(American and World Middleweight Champion)
"CAN DO" CURRY SHRIMP ON RICE

2 cups cooked white rice
Dash oregano
Dash salt
1 pound large shrimp, cooked and peeled
Dash curry powder
Dash cayenne pepper
1 tomato, sliced

1. Sprinkle rice with oregano and dash of salt.
2. Sprinkle shrimp with curry powder and cayenne pepper.
3. Surround shrimp with rice and sliced tomatoes and serve.

Serves 4

Per serving: 223 calories, 23 grams protein, 28 grams carbohydrate, 1.2 grams fat.

Gladys Portugues
(Night-of-the-Champions Winner)
PORTUGUES TUNA ON RICE

1 7-ounce can water-packed tuna, drained and rinsed
    twice
⅛ teaspoon oregano
Dash pepper
Dash dried dill
Lettuce leaves
1 cup cooked white rice
Steamed broccoli (about 1 pound fresh or 1 10-ounce
    package frozen)

1. Place tuna in bowl and mix with oregano, pepper, and
   dill.
2. Place lettuce leaves on 2 plates and fill with tuna
   mixture.
3. Surround lettuce leaves with rice.
4. Surround rice with a ring of broccoli spears.

Serves 2

**Per serving: 268 calories, 33.3 grams protein, 30.3 grams
carbohydrate, 1.2 grams fat.**

BEEF DISH

Mohamed Makkawy
(IFBB Pro Grand Prix Champion)
MOHAMED'S LONDON LIFTING HIGH

¼ teaspoon dried bell peppers
½ cup white wine
¼ cup water
¼ teaspoon garlic powder
¼ cup chopped onion
¼ teaspoon oregano
1½ pounds lean London broil

1. Combine bell peppers, white wine, water, garlic powder, onion, and oregano.
2. Let meat soak in marinade for 3 hours, covered, at room temperature.
3. Broil London broil to taste, pouring marinade over the meat every 3 minutes.

Serves 4

Per serving: 523 calories, 27 grams protein, 2 grams carbohydrate, 42 grams fat.

PASTA AND GRAIN DISHES
Debbie Basile
(American Lightweight Champion)
POWERLIFT PASTA SALAD

1 cup whole wheat pasta
2 cloves garlic
½ tablespoon olive oil
1 medium-sized zucchini, chopped
½ green pepper, chopped
⅓ cup water
½ cup frozen peas, cooked
½ tablespoon Romano cheese
4 cherry tomatoes

1. Cook pasta in 1 quart water and drain.
2. Saute garlic in oil and remove with slotted spoon. Set aside on paper napkin to absorb excess oil.
3. Steam zucchini and green pepper in ⅓ cup water for 5 minutes.
4. Mix pasta, zucchini, green pepper, peas, and garlic together.
5. Sprinkle with cheese and garnish with cherry tomatoes.

Serves 1

Per serving: 255 calories, 13 grams protein, 48 grams carbohydrate, 2.5 grams fat.

Pillow
(Gold's Classic Champion, Ms. Alaska)
PILLOW'S BREAKFAST BOMBER

1 ounce oatmeal
¾ cup water
3 egg whites
¼ cup water
½ teaspoon vanilla extract
1 1-gram package Sweet 'n Low

1. Bring oatmeal and ¾ cup water to boil.
2. Place egg whites, ¼ cup water, and vanilla extract in blender and blend at medium speed until slightly stiff.
3. Add to boiling water and oatmeal and cook until thickened.
4. Add Sweet 'n Low.

Serves 1

Per serving: 71 calories, 11 grams protein, 4 grams carbohydrate, 3 grams fat.

DESSERT DISHES

Robby Robinson
(Mr. America, Mr. Universe)
ROBINSON'S STRIATIONS FRUIT SALAD

1 cup sliced strawberries
¼ honeydew melon, cubed
¼ cantaloupe, cubed
½ grapefruit, peeled and cut into sections

1. Place all fruits in mixing bowl.
2. Toss and serve.

Serves 2

Per serving: 113 calories, 2 grams protein, 27 grams carbohydrate, 1 gram fat.

Sue Ann McKean
(Superbowl of Bodybuilding Champion)
ANAEROBIC RICE PUDDING

1⅓ cups skim milk
⅛ teaspoon salt
¼ cup natural honey
1 tablespoon soft butter
1 teaspoon vanilla
5 eggs
2 cups cooked brown rice
½ teaspoon grated lemon rind
1 teaspoon lemon juice
1 cup raisins
Dash ground cinnamon
Dash ground nutmeg

1. Combine milk, salt, honey, butter, vanilla, eggs, and rice.
2. Add lemon rind, lemon juice, and raisins and combine with a fork.
3. Place in a nonstick baking dish and sprinkle with cinnamon and nutmeg.
4. Bake in a preheated 325°F oven for 50 minutes.

Serves 4

Per serving: 481 calories, 13 grams protein, 90 grams carbohydrate, 11 grams fat.

Rick Wayne
(Mr. World, Pro Mr. America)
RICKY'S CARIBBEAN FRUITY RICE

½ papaya, chopped fine
1 slice pineapple, diced
¼ avocado, chopped fine
3 tomatoes
2 cups cooked rice
1 cup low-fat vanilla yogurt
1 tablespoon coconut flakes

1. Mix papaya, pineapple, avocado, and tomatoes to-gether and blend into rice.
2. Fold in yogurt.
3. Pour into dessert dishes and sprinkle with coconut.
4. Refrigerate overnight and serve.

Serves 4

Per serving: 233 calories, 7 grams protein, 45 grams carbohydrate, 4 grams fat.

THICK SHAKES AND BEVERAGES

Samir Bannout
(1983 Mr. Olympia)
SAMIR'S VANILLA YOGURT SHAKE

1 cup plain low-fat yogurt
¼ cup Perrier
¼ teaspoon vanilla extract
Dash ground cinnamon

1. Place yogurt and Perrier in mixing bowl.
2. Beat mixture with spoon until you have an even consistency.
3. Add vanilla extract and dash of cinnamon.
4. Beat again until smooth.

5. Pour into glass and serve or refrigerate and serve later.

Serves 1

Per serving: 144 calories, 16 grams protein, 12 grams carbohydrate, 3.5 grams fat.

Bill Pearl
(Mr. America, Mr. USA, Four-Time Mr. Universe)
BILL PEARL'S FASTING JUICES

Fasting Juice 1
1 quart grapefruit juice
1 quart water

Pour grapefruit juice and water into large container and mix well. Drink 1 glass every few hours and drink water in between juices.

Serves 1 for a day

Per serving: 392 calories, 4.8 grams protein, 92 grams carbohydrate, 0.8 grams fat.

Fasting Juice 2
1 quart orange juice
1 quart water

Pour orange juice and water into large container and mix well. Drink 1 glass every few hours and drink water in between juices.

Serves 1 for a day

Per serving: 448 calories, 6.8 grams protein, 103 grams carbohydrate, 2 grams fat.

Fasting Juice 3
1 quart V8 juice
1 quart water

Pour V8 juice and water into large container and mix well.
    Drink 1 glass every few hours and drink water in
    between juices. *Note:* V8 has a high sodium content.
    Do not use before a contest.

Serves 1 for a day

**Per serving: 184 calories, 8.8 grams protein, 41.6 grams
carbohydrate, .8 grams fat.**

MEAL PLANS OF THE CHAMPIONS
Clarence Bass
(Past 40 Mr. USA)

Breakfast
1 cup cereal
1 cup skim milk
3 eggs
1 slice whole wheat toast

Lunch
Peanut butter sandwich (2 slices whole wheat toast, 4
    tablespoons peanut butter)
1 cup yogurt

Snack
1 apple
1 pear
¼ cup raisins

Dinner
3 eggs
1 slice whole wheat bread
1 cup skim milk
Large green salad

Snack
Protein drink
  1 cup milk
  1 cup water
  1 raw egg
  1 scoop milk and egg protein powder
  Natural fiber from psyllium seed husks

Tim Belknap
(Mr. America)

Tim Belknap is a diabetic, so he must eat frequently. (He also uses assorted food supplements—vitamin B complex, C, E; multiminerals; chelated individual minerals; electrolyte replacement drinks; etc.)

Breakfast
5 egg whites, hard-boiled
2 slices 7-grain whole wheat toast
1 teaspoon honey

Snack
1 banana

Snack
1 baked potato

Lunch
7 ounces water-packed tuna

Dinner
2 small chicken breasts, broiled

Snack
1½ cups 7-grain cereal, hot

Late Dinner
6 ounces red snapper
Salad (no dressing)
1 baked potato

Lydia Cheng
(Big Apple, Tri-State, East Coast Championships)

Breakfast
Scrambled eggs (2 egg whites, ½ cup mushrooms, and 1 chopped scallion, scrambled together in a nonstick pan)

Snack
½ cup fresh pineapple

Lunch
6 ounces scrod, broiled
Lettuce and cucumber salad (with balsamic vinegar mixed with salt-free mustard, ⅛ cup grapefruit juice, and assorted herbs and spices)
1 cup steamed asparagus

Dinner
6 ounces chicken breast, broiled
1 cup steamed zucchini
Lettuce and cucumber salad with balsamic vinegar dressing (see above)
1 cup steamed asparagus

Snack
¼ cantaloupe

Laura Combes
(First American Women's Bodybuilding Champion)

Snack
½ cantaloupe
Black coffee
Food supplements

Breakfast
4 egg whites
1 slice 7-grain toast
10–15 free-form amino acid capsules
Iced tea

Lunch
8 ounces fish, broiled
Green vegetable
½ cup rice
Black coffee
Food supplements

Snack
1 apple
10–15 free-form amino acid capsules

Dinner
8 ounces fish, broiled
Green vegetables
Black coffee

Candy Csencsits
(Miss Eastern America, 2nd Place Miss Olympia)

Breakfast
4 egg whites
½ cantaloupe
1 slice whole-grain bread
Bottled water
Vitamin supplements

Snack
Bottled water

Lunch
Chicken salad (broiled white-meat chicken, lettuce,
   cucumbers, herbs and spices)
Steamed string beans
Iced tea

Snack
Bottled water

Dinner
8 ounces flounder, broiled
Peas and carrots (frozen, cooked)
Any raw vegetable
Iced tea

Dawn Marie Gnaegi
(USA Middleweight Champion)

Breakfast
2 eggs, scrambled (1 yolk, 2 whites)
½ grapefruit
Herb tea

Lunch
Tuna pasta salad (4 ounces tuna, soya-rice pasta, 1
    tablespoon Haines eggless mayonnaise, chopped
    celery, onion)
Herb tea

Dinner
4 ounces chicken, skinned and boiled
1 small baked potato
Herb tea

Snacks
Distilled water
Herb tea
Multivitamin tablets
Potassium tablets

Mohamed Makkawy
(Mr. Universe, Mr. International)

Breakfast
Distilled water (minimum amount)

Lunch (the only meal of the day)
12 ounces steak

Dinner
Distilled water (minimum amount)

Matt Mendenhall
(Runner-up, American Championships)

Breakfast
Protein drink and puffed rice (Crystal Light, 1 banana, 1
    cup frozen strawberries, 2 tablespoons psyllium husks,

3 tablespoons 100 percent egg protein powder, and
   crushed ice; blended well and poured over puffed rice)
Multipack vitamins

Snack
2 apples
15–25 free-form amino acid capsules

Lunch
Tuna sandwich (8 ounces low-sodium water-packed
   tuna, mixed with 2 tablespoons low-calorie Thousand
   Island dressing and 2 tablespoons plain low-fat yogurt,
   served on 2 slices whole wheat bread)
1 multipack vitamins and minerals

Snack
Same as breakfast but without puffed rice

Dinner
2 chicken breasts, skinned and steamed
1 head cauliflower, steamed and sprinkled with Butter
   Buds
1 multipack vitamins and minerals

Snack
½ cantaloupe

Steve Michalik
(Mr. America)

Breakfast
1 cup cooked oatmeal
1 cup fresh pineapple
1 cup black coffee

Snack
8 ounces white-meat chicken, broiled
8 ounces distilled water

Lunch
8 ounces flounder, broiled
Iced tea

Dinner
6 egg whites, hard-boiled
8–20 amino acids (crystallized capsules)

Gladys Portugues
(Night-of-the-Champions Winner)

Breakfast
2 scrambled eggs
1 cooked potato (fried in a nonstick pan with a little oil)
1 slice whole wheat bread

Snack
1 papaya

Lunch
7 ounces water-packed tuna, drained and rinsed
4 ounces pasta
Salad (tomato, lettuce, cucumber)
Assorted steamed vegetables

Snack
2 apples

Dinner
10 ounces chicken, skinned and broiled
Assorted steamed vegetables
Fruit salad (assorted fruits)
Salad with natural vinegar

Snacks
Assorted fruit juices during the day

15

SAMPLE MEAL PLANS

In the previous chapters, we have given you a variety of recipes. In this chapter, we give you a sample week's meal plans (one for women and one for men). These meal plans are designed to show you how to reduce your caloric intake gradually so that you do not shock your body when trying to reduce body fat and body weight.

You will note that the reduction is approximately 75 calories a day for women and 100 calories a day for men. We start the women at 1,800 calories and the men at 3,000 calories.

Naturally, you will want to adjust the plans to your particular body type. Some women eat as many as 2,500 calories a day and will reduce from that point, while others eat as few as 1,500 and will have to reduce from that point. The same idea, of course, applies to the men.

We do not suggest that you reduce your calories by more than 100 a day unless, of course, you are on a "crash" diet because you foolishly postponed dieting. Most of us have found ourselves in this unfortunate situation at least once in our lives, and if this happens to you, you will probably make sure it never happens again, because quick drops in caloric intake exact a heavy toll on the body.

A WEEK OF MEAL PLANS FOR WOMEN

See index for page numbers of all recipes.

Day One

	Calories
Breakfast	
Scrambled Eggs and Veggies	169
Pineapple-Lemon Lift	167
Snack	
Muscle Mass Banana Shake	247
Lunch	
Big Bill's Sloppy Gyms	263
Esthetic Vegetable Rice	141
Fruit Quintets	174
Dinner	
Creamed Chicken	254
Orange Energy	85
Hard/Soft Apple Bread Pudding	312
	1,812

Day Two

	Calories
Breakfast	
Phantom's Waffles and Strawberries	165
Snack	
Raspberry-Pineapple Parfaits	111
Lunch	
Power Workout Spinach and Cottage Cheese	114
Crab and Avocado Salad	267
Snack	
Coconut-Peach Salad	112
Dinner	
Caraco Carrots and Applesauce	146

Baked Salmon with Lemon	492
Lettuce Salad	10
Garden Dressing	122

Snack

Six Fruits Salad	<u>205</u>
	1,744

Day Three

Breakfast	*Calories*
Training Partner Potato Pancakes	200
Broiled Grapefruit Grasps	100

Snack

Tomato-Pineapple Vinaigrette	71

Lunch

Gorilla Chicken Gumbo Soup	285
Cantonese Shrimp and Snow Peas	209

Dinner

Level III Turkey Roast	430
Gravy	53
IFBB Sweet Potatoes	76
Orange and Cauliflower Superset Salad	70

Snack

Eggnog	<u>151</u>
	1,645

Day Four

Breakfast	*Calories*
Whole Wheat Cheese and Tomato Rounds	199
Sherry Grapefruit	46

Snack

Orange-Cress Salad	89

Lunch
Sole Seviche   327
Popeye's Platter   59

Snack
Red Pepper Salad   51
French Dressing (3 tablespoons)   45

Dinner
The Crane's Ginger Chicken   394
Power Potatoes   171
String Bean and Mushroom Combo   69

Snack
Broiled Fruit Kebabs   <u>118</u>
    1,568

Day Five

	Calories
Breakfast	
Oatmeal with Bananas and Cinnamon	224
Snack	
Orange Banana Thick Shake	311
Lunch	
Chilled Tuna and Rice with Tomatoes	242
Eggplant and Zucchini Medley	78
Snack	
Big Apple Beauty	125
Dinner	
Lucky and Lean Veal Parmesan	286
Asparagus Frittata	83
Dilled Tomatoes and Onions	27
Snack	
Onstage Highball	<u>133</u>
	1,509

Day Six

	Calories
Breakfast	
First-Place Fluffy Omelette	24
Lunch	
Champion Chicken Stew	438
Snack	
Pizza	364
Dinner	
Beef Manicotti	500
Dill-Grilled Tomatoes	35
Snack	
Stuffed Zucchini	66
	1,427

Day Seven

	Calories
Breakfast	
Bran Muffins	95
Snack	
Orange and Cauliflower Superset Salad	70
Lunch	
Fabulous Fruity Chicken	382
Prone Carrot Pudding	148
Snack	
Melon Strawberry Cherry Sweets	112
Dinner	
Broiled Sole Veronique	188
Baked Potatoes with Cottage Cheese	215
Snack	
Pineapple Boats	134
	1,344

A WEEK OF MEAL PLANS FOR MEN

See index for page numbers of recipes.

Day One

Breakfast	*Calories*
Eggnog (2 servings)	302
Broiled Grapefruit Grasps (2 servings)	200
Snack	
Pineapple-Lemon Lift	167
Lunch	
Pita Chicken	370
Potato Salad	215
Snack	
Easy Cheesy Pinwheel Appetizers (3 servings)	350
Dinner	
Veal Chops Mozzarella	922
Tomato-Pineapple Vinaigrette	71
Brussels Sprout and Tomato Salad	37
Snack	
Big Blast Blender Drink, banana (3 ounces powder)	370
	3,004

Day Two

Breakfast	*Calories*
Over-Easy Jumping Jacks	201
Big Blast Blender Drink, cherry (3 ounces powder)	355
Snack	
Power Workout Spinach and Cottage Cheese	114
Lunch	
Off-Season Chicken	603
Chilled Fruit and Rice Salad	214

Snack

Six Fruits Salad (2 servings)	410

Dinner

Big-Time Beef Burgundy	588
Broccoli Boufant	147

Snack

Three-Bean Salad	271
	2,903

Day Three

Breakfast	*Calories*
Spinach and Cheese Pie	616
Sherry Grapefruit	46

Lunch

Salmon Salad with Artichokes	566
Champion Spaghetti and White Wine	335

Snack

Tuna Fruit Salad	345

Dinner

Veal Stew with Rosemary	436
Mashed Potatoes	114

Snack

Precontest Hamburger Pickup	342
	2,800

Day Four

Breakfast	*Calories*
Chilled Fruit and Rice Salad	214
Muscle Mass Banana Shake	247
First Place Fluffy Omelette	24

Snack

Tuna Trade-Off	168

Lunch
Baked Salmon with Lemon   492
Kidney Beans and Brown Rice   302
Creamed Broccoli Soup   89

Snack
Crab and Avocado Salad   267

Dinner
Monster Mushroom Moussaka   443
Intermediate Mashed Potatoes   125
Asparagus Fatburners   10

Snack
Hard/Soft Apple Bread Pudding   312
                                                         2,693

Day Five

Breakfast   *Calories*
Universal Low-Fat Ricotta Cheese (2 servings)   344
2 slices protein bread   90
Sherry Grapefruit   46

Snack
Six Fruits Salad   205

Lunch
Baked Stuffed Pepper   469
Vegetable Cutlet   85
Orange and Cauliflower Superset Salad   70
Creamy Fruit Salad Dressing (3 tablespoons)   111

Snack
Total Body Beef Pizza   375

Dinner
Whitefish Rounds with Dill   399
Scalloped Potatoes   200
Eggplant Parmigiana   204
                                                        2,598

Day Six

	Calories
Breakfast	
Blueberry and Cottage Cheese Insanity	154
Raspberry-Pineapple Parfaits	111
Lunch	
Fish Cakes	517
Baked Potatoes with Cottage Cheese	215
Snack	
Brandy Banana Pumper	169
Dinner	
Big-Time Beef Burgundy	588
Wild Rice with Mushrooms	202
Task Master Apple Pudding	374
Snack	
Pineapple-Lemon Lift	167
	2,497

Day Seven

	Calories
Breakfast	
Hash Browns	148
First Place Fluffy Omelette	24
Snack	
Samir's Vanilla Yogurt Shake	144
Lunch	
Poached Dill Salmon	492
Spinach-Mushroom Salad	46
Snack	
Checklist Chili	446
Dinner	
Superstar Sirloin Tip	588
Easy Eggplant Parmesan	305
Snack	
Six Fruits Salad	205
	2,398

Andreas Cahling.

16
THE VEGETARIAN ALTERNATIVE

There are four classes of vegetarians. *Vegans* are the most fundamental type of vegetarian. They eat only foods from vegetable sources and eschew the use of eggs and/or milk products. *Lacto-vegetarians* eat the same foods as vegans but also include milk and milk products in their diet. *Ovo-vegetarians* eat the same foods as vegans but also include eggs in their diet. And *lacto-ovo-vegetarians* eat the same foods as vegans but include eggs, milk, and milk products in their diet.

You may be forestalled from following a vegetarian diet by the low-protein content of the regimen. You shouldn't worry about this, however, according to **Bill Pearl** (Mr. America, Mr. USA, and four-time NABBA Mr. Universe). Pearl notes, "A growing bodybuilder simply doesn't need 300–400 grams of protein per day to reach his potential. If the protein is from a natural source and is cooked as little as possible, the human body can survive very comfortably—even grow—on only 50–70 grams per day. Furthermore, this protein does not need to be meat, poultry, or fish but can come from vegetable or dairy foods. Beef is actually fairly low in protein because, once you remove all of the fiber, water, and uric acid from a prime steak, very little protein remains.

"If a bodybuilder is eating 300–400 grams of protein per day and is cutting his calories in preparation for a competition, he is bound to become fatigued and lethargic. As a result, the body must take protein and try to convert it to blood sugar to train on—a long process that consumes almost as much energy as it produces. If the bodybuilder doesn't have enough energy with which to train, why take in so much protein?

"The hypothetical bodybuilder I'm discussing would be far better off ingesting half or one-quarter of the protein he's eating, replacing the deleted meat calories with carbohydrate foods for energy. Carbohydrates are the body's preferred source of energy fuel, and anyone who eats an adequate supply of fresh fruit will have an abundance of training energy.

"There's absolutely no question that it is possible to build a high-class physique and be a vegetarian at the same time. Andreas Cahling did it, and I reached great condition at age 50 doing the same thing. Another prime example is Roy Hilligen, a former Mr. America, who at 54 years of age placed very high in the Mr. International competition. Roy has been a vegetarian as long as I've known him, and I met the guy about 1949 or 1950.

"Steve Reeves was about as close to being a vegetarian as anyone I have known, and he's one of the most revered athletes in bodybuilding history. Steve was almost exclusively a lacto-vegetarian, and he ate only minor amounts of meat. During the times I ate out with him, Reeves was always eating salads, avocados, fresh fruits, fresh vegetables, plus some occasional milk products.

"I've personally been a strict lacto-vegetarian since 1971 and a semivegetarian since about 1963 or 1964. Back in the '60s, I was working with the astronauts and company executives at North American Rockwell. I was telling these people all about good health. We were taking treadmill tests, and I was knocking these guys dead.

"One day—just as a lark—the doctor checked my cholesterol level. It was 307, an unbelievably high level, so my blood was running almost as thick as syrup through my veins. The doctor said, 'I don't give a damn how good you look, Bill, or how big your arm is. You're asking for trouble!' He went on to tell me I could die just as easily at 50 as anyone else, even though I felt I was in great shape. Naturally, that started me thinking.

"Because of bodybuilding, I was somewhat afraid to stop eating meats, but after the doctor told me this and I had successfully competed in the 1967 Mr. Universe, I decided to change my eating habits. Becoming a lacto-vegetarian was my response to the situation, and except for a short period of meat eating before my last Universe in 1971, I've been a vegetarian since 1967. In 1971, I simply wasn't convinced I could do it again without meat, but at past 50 years of age and more than 10 years later I've reached great shape on a lacto-vegetarian diet."

Cahling actually gained faster as a vegetarian than as a carnivore: "Once I went completely lacto-vegetarian, I noticed I was feeling much better. My energy was higher, and I was really blasting through my workouts. As a result, I began making unbelievable muscle gains all of the time while keeping my body fat levels lower than they'd ever been in the off-season."

"Vegetarian eating has had numerous positive effects on my body," notes Pearl. "My cholesterol gradually dropped down to a normal level of 198, and my blood pressure was markedly lowered. My pulse rate and other physiological processes are much better now, and overall I'm in better shape in my 50s than I was in my 20s.

"One of the most dramatic changes has been in my uric acid levels. My uric acid is now down to zero, but before becoming a vegetarian it was so sky-high that every joint in my body ached. My uric acid was once so high that I could hardly move my hands. I actually thought I was getting arthritis!

"Today my energy levels are incredible, and I feel like a million dollars all of the time. There's nobody I've ever trained with whom I couldn't stay up with in a hard workout. My energy is greater than ever, and they don't need to knock off 15 cows a year to keep me fed! Those cows are conceivably just as important on earth as any human being.

"The biggest change, however, has been in my attitude toward myself and my fellow man. Perhaps this sounds crazy, but I'm not nearly as aggressive as I have been in the past. There have been times in my life that I've wanted to go out and fight some guy for saying something that offended me. Or I'd scream and holler and really make an ass out of myself. Now I catch myself smiling and trying to work out a problem. Vegetarianism has definitely had a mellowing effect on me."

Andreas Cahling has also noticed the calming effect of his vegetarian diet. "I used to be pretty irritable and touchy, particularly in the last few weeks before a competition, when I was eating beef, chicken, and fish," Andreas notes. "Once I became a complete vegetarian—which was a gradual process—I became less and less jumpy. I even began to find it easier to fall asleep each night, which I couldn't do when I was eating flesh.

"To show you the dramatic effect of eating flesh—at least on my body—just eating a few pieces of sushi with a small amount of seafood in it can set me back to square one emotionally. I become very irritable for a couple of days. Having lived in Japan for a year, I have a real taste for sushi, but in order to preserve my sanity and personal comfort I have to avoid eating this tasty delicacy!"

With reservation, **Bill Pearl** agrees with Cahling's contention that vegetarianism can increase longevity: "It's difficult to determine these things, but I feel vegetarianism promotes longevity. But even if I die at 55 or 60, my life has been vastly improved by vegetarian eating. Right now I'm up every morning at 3:45 A.M. and I seldom go to bed before 10:00 P.M. Every hour of my day is filled completely, and I'm moving 100 miles per hour all of the time."

Despite the overwhelming benefits of adopting a vegetarian lifestyle, Bill Pearl notes that there are a couple of drawbacks. "It's sometimes difficult to be invited out to people's homes to eat," he confesses, "because they tend to be uneasy about what to feed you. It's a little easier to entertain at your home, but some individuals are wary of coming over to eat what they feel will be 18 pounds of rabbit food.

"Whenever you travel away from home, you'll end up in restaurants eating mostly eggs and salads. I usually have a difficult time once I leave home, but it's not so inconvenient as to make me eat steak and hamburgers."

Andreas Cahling has solved the problem of eating away

from home. "I travel quite a bit to compete, give training seminars, and present posing exhibitions," he says. "I can always find a good salad bar at my hotel and even order a vegetarian meal on the plane if I call ahead. Still, I carry food with me on trips for snacks and to tide me over in emergencies when I can't find the right restaurant at which to eat. For a day, cheese will keep without spoiling, so I pack a little of my favorite goat's milk cheese. Favorite nonperishable foods that I carry are various seeds and nuts, plus a few slices of flourless bread. This technique works really well."

Even though Andreas has squatted with 700 pounds and benched 440 for reps, the general consensus is that vegetarian bodybuilders are not quite as strong as their carnivore counterparts. "Yes, some experts feel that vegetarians aren't as strong as meat eaters," concedes **Bill Pearl.** "While they may not be as strong in terms of the amount of weight they can push, vegetarians have a great deal more endurance than the average bodybuilder. And just because a bodybuilder can push more weight doesn't mean he'll end up with more muscle. Weight counts, but so does the intensity of a workout, and intensity comes from how you feel the weight in an exercise and from how little you rest between sets when using maximum loads in all of your movements."

Cahling believes the fears of some bodybuilders that they can't build a high degree of muscle mass on a vegetarian regimen are unfounded. He notes, "My best competitive weight on an omnivorous regimen was 177 pounds at the 1978 IFBB Mr. Universe competitions in Acapulco. Shortly after that I turned completely vegetarian and began to make much better gains. My peak competitive weight at 5'7" in height by early 1984 was 198 pounds at the Pro World Championships. And I was absolutely shredded at that weight.

"So, in five and a half years, I gained 21 pounds of pure muscle, an average of just under 5 pounds per year. That might not sound like much of a gain each year, but any champion bodybuilder would be overjoyed with a similar gain in pure muscle mass. Four or 5 pounds of muscle mass can literally transform the appearance of your physique."

Because Bill Pearl's body weight fell from 240 to only 185 after becoming a full vegetarian in 1971, it would appear that the diet prevented him from being massively muscled. Bill disagrees: "Actually, my weight losses after the 1971 Universe are totally misleading and unrelated to vegetarianism. Back in '71 I was totally fed up with competing. Indeed, I hadn't even wanted to compete in the '71 Universe, but everyone was badgering me about competing against Arnold Schwarzenegger. So, even at 41 years of age, I finally decided to give everyone a last shot at me. But after that was finished—due to my distaste for being pushed into competing—I never wanted to be in a similar position again. Even though I won the '71 NABBA Mr. Universe title, I vowed never to compete again.

"When it was over with, I didn't care about the trophy, the title, or anything else, except being left alone. I figured that if I just totally ignored the sport—didn't even pose at exhibitions—and if I could change my image to look like a nonbodybuilder, I'd get some peace and quiet. So, I began bicycle riding and fasting for weeks at a time to reduce my body weight. I wanted to weigh as little as possible so people would forget about me as a bodybuilder, which is exactly what happened.

"Then I was invited to guest-pose at the 1978 Mr. America show on the 25th anniversary of winning that title myself. The idea intrigued me, so I decided to go for it. Even though I was on a strict vegetarian regimen, I added weight quite easily. It was simply a matter of eating more calories—not necessarily more protein—and training heavier in the gym. Others have done the same thing. Although he does eat some chicken and fish, Mike Mentzer reached his most massive and ripped shape when consuming less than 70 grams of protein per day prior to a show."

Cahling's conversion to lacto-vegetarianism was gradual. "I used to eat all of the flesh foods—beef, pork, chicken, turkey, lamb, fish," Mr. International recalls. "My workouts were sluggish all of the time, but I didn't understand that the meat was causing my lethargy. My skin broke out a lot, and I had extreme difficulty in getting ripped up for each of my competitions.

"Initially, I dropped beef and pork from my diet, because they were so fatty that their high caloric content was keeping my own body fat levels too high. Oddly, I noticed that I also began to feel a little better, so I studied a few nutrition books. I was startled to learn how many steroids and other hormones were being shot into cattle and hogs to get their weight up. I didn't want that in my body, so I haven't touched beef or pork since then.

"About a year later I dropped poultry from my diet as well, because chickens and turkeys are also pumped full of hormones. And as I dropped beef, pork, and poultry from my diet, I correspondingly increased my intake of fresh vegetables, fruit, milk products, grains, nuts, and seeds.

"Gradually, I ate fish less frequently each week and consumed progressively smaller quantities each time I ate fish. Finally, I was down to a sushi meal once every couple of weeks. I was feeling so good at this point and making such great gains from my sessions in the gym that I decided to go completely vegetarian. Believe me, it's the best decision of my life!"

Bill Pearl does not suggest that a bodybuilder go on a lacto-vegetarian—or any type of vegetarian—diet unless he has a firm conviction to do so. Says Mr. Universe, "It's just like a religion or any other way of life. A vegetarian diet takes time to pay dividends, and to go on and off every few months is equivalent to stopping and starting smoking. You might as well have never stopped in the first place.

"I wouldn't presume to tell you to change to a vegetarian lifestyle, but if the concept interests you, I'd suggest you read as many books as possible on the subject before making up your mind. Why do you want to do this? Is it for humanitarian reasons—do you not like to have animals killed to feed you? Is it for health? One of the best books I have read on the subject is *Are You Confused?* by Paava Ariola (Health Plus/Contemporary, 1971). That book probably did as much to convert me to vegetarianism as anything I've ever read."

The Pearl of the Universe also doesn't presume to tell

lacto-vegetarian bodybuilders what to eat. He reveals, "I can only tell you how I eat, and you can take it from there. When I get up at 3:45 in the morning to train—which suits my lifestyle—I might have a cup of mint tea as a perker-upper. Once back at home from the gym, I may have a cheese omelette or five or six eggs prepared in some other way. I might also have a little cottage cheese, some heavy type of bran bread with butter, and another cup of tea.

"For lunch I'll have a large fresh salad, putting the widest possible variety of salad ingredients into it. The only dressing might be a small amount of oil and vinegar.

"At night my wife will cook up some type of a souffle, or perhaps a casserole. I'll have another fresh salad and for dessert maybe some yogurt or fruit. My supplements include a good B complex, C, E, kelp, and zinc. I think that after the age of 40–45 zinc is very important for gland health. And that's my total diet."

Andreas Cahling revealed his vegetarian diet as well: "One of the staples of my diet is grilled cheese sandwiches. I take one slice of heavy, whole-grain bread and slap on a thick slab of raw goat cheese. Then I lightly toast this in the oven to melt the cheese into the bread. I may eat four or five of these open-faced sandwiches per day.

"Salads—especially those with a lot of sprouts, mush-rooms, and tomatoes—are also a staple in my diet. I always eat these raw and without any dressing. A medium-sized fresh salad is a gastronomical delight, and you won't even miss the dressing.

"I also eat a few nuts, some fruit, freshly squeezed fruit and vegetable juices, and perhaps some sunflower and pumpkin seeds during the day. Juices are very cleansing, especially green juices like celery, parsley, and spinach. I don't use steroids, but anyone who does would be a fool not to cleanse his body with juices periodically when on steroids.

"Because of my fresh and natural diet, I don't seem to need many food supplements. Just before a contest I'll take low-potency natural vitamins and minerals. You must be very careful in selecting supplements since so many today include petroleum derivatives. Read your labels carefully and, if you don't know a particular ingredient, don't buy the supplement."

We asked Bill Pearl if he would ever revert to eating meat. "No," he answered. "Once you're eating as a vegetarian, you can't be swayed away from it by anyone or anything regardless of the situation. If a person offered me $50,000 to eat a steak, I'd tell him to stick it in his pocket. What's the sense of making a commitment if you're not committed? I'm a firm believer in sticking to my convictions!"

FASTING

We will discuss the topic of fasting in this chapter because many vegetarian athletes take periodic fasts to cleanse and detoxify their systems. It's a good practice that even nonvegetarians should use from time to time, particularly if they take anabolic steroids prior to a competition.

"If a person is in very good condition and he knows his diet is not lacking in vitamins and minerals," instructs **Bill Pearl,** "I think fasting would be beneficial. However, for a person habitually on junk foods—hamburgers, hot dogs, soft drinks, candy bars, etc.—a fast could be detrimental because he'd be depriving his body of even more essential nutrients.

"A fast of one day per week would be one of the healthiest things a bodybuilder could do because it gives the body's glands and internal organs a chance to rest. I personally recommend fasting on juices. Take vegetable and fruit juices, dilute them 50 percent with pure water, and drink about a half gallon of diluted juice each day. This will clean out your system and let your body physiologically rest."

Many top bodybuilders have fasted for short periods of time on just water, but all have reported dissatisfaction with such an extreme fast. According to **Rachel McLish** (Pro World Champion and twice Miss Olympia), "I fasted on just water before a show when I was behind on my peaking schedule. The constant hunger was agonizing, and I ended up losing mostly muscle mass on the fast. I'll never do it again."

Erica Mes (IFBB Lightweight World Champion) reported similar problems with fasting on just water. "The only benefit for me was a cleansing of my system," she recalls, "as well as a small fat loss. But the fat loss was accompanied by a loss of muscle mass. Overall the extreme fast on just water was an unpleasant experience for me."

Among high-level bodybuilders currently competing, **Andreas Cahling** is the leading practitioner of fasting for rejuvenation and improved bodybuilding gains. We are fortunate that this great IFBB Mr. International winner spoke at length with us on the subject of fasting.

"Man is a slow learner," Andreas began. "Neither nature itself nor irrefutable history seems able to convince him that sometimes *not* eating is healthful. Instead, bodybuilders continue to gorge themselves with every food available and suffer all sorts of problems as a result—protein overdoses, hypoglycemia, obesity, etc.—not to mention that they bring their quest for greater muscle mass and better muscularity to a shuddering halt.

"Yet all of the evidence is there. Wild animals not only are able to heal themselves without drugs, but they do not suffer from being overweight. Since creation, nature has been beating us over the head with the fact that animals have always instinctively avoided food when feeling ill. To these so-called lower animals, a decreased appetite during disease is an alarm signal, telling them to starve a fever rather than feed it. Still, we can't seem to grasp that. We continue to flaunt our favorite maxim of conceit: Man is the only rational animal. Of course, that's man's definition, not animals'.

"As if nature weren't qualified enough as a teacher, we've also failed to grasp the message of thousands of years of history. Even before the age of tribal medicine men, fasting was used to cure diseases and rejuvenate the body. Hippocrates, the Father of Medicine, recommended fasting, while Socrates and Plato used fasting to obtain physical and mental highs.

"The Greeks were not alone in their respect for fasting. Philosophers and yogis of the Orient—known for longevity and mental activity as well as spiritual consciousness—

practiced fasting. And American Plains Indians used fasting as a means of cleansing their bodies and inducing spiritual visions.

"The logic behind fasting is convincing. Let's start with the late Hans Selye, MD, the renowned Canadian researcher and author. Dr. Selye's concept is basic: a person is as young or old as his smallest vital component, the cell; therefore, to maintain youth and health, our bodies must constantly be producing more new cells to replace dead cells.

"Unfortunately, when we allow waste products to build up in our bodies, these products interfere with the growth of new cells by inhibiting the transportation of nutrients. To resist aging, not only must we promote the building of new cells, but we must also eliminate aged and dead cells from our bodies as quickly as possible."

Above all else, fasting is a superior source of body rejuvenation, making your digestive system and other internal functions much more efficient. Cahling continues, "Fasting becomes necessary when there is no longer an effective means of rapidly clearing out cellular waste to provide a healthful environment for new cells.

"How can something as simple as abstinence from food provide such positive results? During a prolonged fast—more than three days—the body lives on its own tissues. Sounds dangerous, particularly for a bodybuilder, doesn't it? Yet, ironically, fasting is probably the most healthful road you can take toward bodybuilding success. Let me tell you why this is true.

"The secret of fasting's effectiveness is that the body is quite selective in the use of its own cells. First, to satisfy its nourishment needs, it starts breaking down and burning the cells that are diseased, degenerated, old, or dead. During a fast, the body feeds on the most unclean and inferior material in the body, such as fat deposits and tumors.

"Cells from important organs, such as the heart, brain, and nervous system, will not be metabolized. The advantage of this process to a bodybuilder is obvious—with the widespread, stupid use of anabolic steroids and a prepossessing lust for getting ripped to the bone, the fast is a means of achieving new muscle tissue, rejuvenated strength, and new cells. I believe fasting is superior to the most sophisticated diets known.

"It's difficult to believe that your body can actually build new cells faster when you limit your nutrient intake, but it's a physiological fact. Fasting requires faith in your body's ability to take care of itself. In fact, if you give it a chance, your body will do a better job of maintaining its own health than you can.

"Even though no protein is consumed during a fast, your blood protein level will remain normal. That's because the protein in your body will be converted from one form to another in order to satisfy specific needs. Amino acids— the building blocks of protein—can be reused time after time to build new cells."

Cahling even believes that fasting can improve physical strength: "Waste products reduce your body's efficiency, so your objective should be to get rid of them as quickly as possible. When you fast, organs such as lungs, kidney, and liver are relieved of their waste loads, freeing them for higher work capacities. That's why you experience re- newed energy during a fast and increased strength shortly after you break a fast. And remember, there's no reason to cut back on your workouts during a prolonged fast. In fact, you can approach them with renewed vigor."

According to **Andreas Cahling,** your mental attitude during a fast can mean the difference between success and failure: "Just remember that there is no relationship between forced starvation and voluntary abstinence from food. Forced starvation carries with it uncertainty and fear, which has a paralyzing effect on body functions and can damage your health.

"However, if you approach fasting with confidence and a full understanding of its benefits, your body, in turn, will respond to this positive attitude.

"Even physical symptoms that seem adverse are actually beneficial results of a fast. For example, after the first two or three days, you might experience a slight headache and mild dizziness. Your skin might even break out. But this just means that the amount of toxins expelled during a fast can be 10 times normal. Try to ignore your anxiety and revel in the cleansing effect of your fast."

Andreas points out that there is a right way and a wrong way to undertake a fast: "For optimum bodybuilding benefits, you should go on a short fast about three months before your next competition. This will stimulate your body's natural anabolism for increased muscle tissue production, while bringing out your cuts and giving you new training energy and motivation.

"If you have been using steroids or other bodybuilding drugs, their effects may linger after you stop taking them, so allow about two months for your body to return to normal before undertaking a fast to cleanse it.

"Since supplements can be assimilated only in combination with food, they should also be curtailed. During a fast you would just be wasting them. The only possible exception might be two or three widely spaced 500-miligram tablets of vitamin C, which significantly assists in the body detoxification process.

"If you have never fasted before, or if you plan on fasting only with water, you should definitely see your physician before initiating your fast. A fruit and vegetable juice fast maintained for a limited time, on the other hand, presents no danger and is something you can begin tomorrow.

"Some individuals might claim that a fast on juices rather than only pure water is not a real fast, but it's actually a superior one. Juices accelerate the body's cleansing capacity by supplying necessary minerals and ionic charges.

"To prepare your body for a juice fast, begin with a two- or three-day diet consisting of only raw fruit and vegetables as well as juices. Eat fruit one meal and juices the next; do not mix fruit and vegetables at the same meal because each requires different enzymes for proper digestion.

"On the fourth day, begin your juice fast and remain on it for four to six days. Gradually, feelings of hunger will disappear. Drink as much juice as you can hold, because this both assists in the cleansing of your body and decreases any sensations of hunger. Carrot, celery, beet, apple, and watermelon juices are all excellent."

While you can purchase reasonably fresh bottled juices at health food stores and supermarkets, you will benefit most from using fresh juice that you've just squeezed yourself. A good juicer is fairly expensive, but in the long run it's well worth the investment.

During a fast, you should take steps to cleanse your lower intestines, which become clogged with deposits of hardened feces and partially digested food. When these deposits lodge in the folds and crevices of your intestines, they can impede the absorption of nutrients that your body can put to good use in building larger, high-quality skeletal muscles.

You should mount a two-pronged attack on these toxic deposits in your digestive tract. First, you can flush out much of this gunk by taking psyllium capsules (three at a time, two or three times per day, followed each time by at least eight ounces of juice or water). Psyllium is a potent natural bulk laxative that absorbs water, expands, and more or less scours these harmful deposits from the walls of your intestines.

Combine psyllium with a special type of enema each morning to further dislodge harmful deposits. Brew up about a quart of chamomile tea and allow the tea to cool to body temperature. Take as much of the tea enema as comfortably possible and hold it for at least five minutes before expelling it. During that period of time, do slow side bends and leg raises to assist the tea to dislodge harmful deposits in your intestines. You simply won't believe some of the gunk this type of enema will dislodge. And soon you'll notice your energy levels beginning to soar.

Actually, one day of juice fasting per month—combined with an enema—will significantly improve your progress in bodybuilding. Try it, and you'll see why so many bodybuilders swear by this program of fasting and enemas.

Once you have fasted for as long as you planned to, you must stop the fast gradually. Explains Andreas Cahling, "The famous health doctor Otto F. Buchinger said, 'Even an idiot can fast, but only a wise man knows how to break a fast.' In other words, the great benefits of a fast can be sabotaged if your return to solid food is not done properly.

"Above all else, you must *gradually* return to your normal diet. And in order to accomplish this, I suggest eating only small amounts of solid food at first, and eat that food slowly, chewing it thoroughly. During this transition period of two or three days, your diet should consist of only raw fruit and vegetables. Then gradually add other foods, but be careful not to eat fatty meats until at least a couple of weeks after you've terminated your fast.

"Perhaps the most important rule of all when fasting is to stay completely away from coffee and all drugs, other than those required to keep a minority of individuals alive. A fast highly sensitizes your body to drugs, and the smallest amounts can seriously damage you.

"I urge you to try fasting. Your first experience will astound you. The fast will change not only the composition of your body but also your mind. Rather than maintaining a body composed of diseased cells and painful poisons, you'll have a body consisting of pure, natural, organic nutrients and fresh, new muscle tissue. And rather than having a mind of self-limiting ego, you'll have fresh, clear brain power. And that's the *only* way to the top!"

Deborah Diana.

17
NUTRITION POTPOURRI

In this chapter, we have included many anecdotes of how the top male and female bodybuilding champions feel about various aspects of bodybuilding diets. Most of these anecdotes have been gleaned from the authors' personal interviews with the various champions. A few others were published in various issues of *Muscle & Fitness* magazine. All anecdotes have been chosen to provide you with a maximum of interesting inside information.

Arnold Schwarzenegger (four-time Mr. Universe, Mr. World, Mr. International, seven-time Mr. Olympia, actor, best-selling author): "I totally agree that you should never go on a zero-carbohydrate diet. The most important thing in bodybuilding nutrition is that you have foods that will keep you healthy, and zero-carb diets are very unhealthy. Healthy foods make you feel good, and feeling good is an essential part of having productive workouts, those three-to five-hour sessions we sometimes have before competition.

"I would suggest eating natural carbohydrates like fructose. Eat a banana, an apple, some vegetables. Cut out the bread, ice cream, cake, cookies, and soft drinks. These carbohydrates are harmful. I believe in low-calorie diets that are balanced enough to include natural carbohydrates.

"I never counted grams of carbohydrate before a contest. Instead, I simply relied on what the mirror told me. If I start on a reduced-calorie diet three months before a contest and after a month progress is being made—the abdominals are coming out and so forth—I'll keep on that same diet. If progress is not as fast as I'd like it, I'll close down a little bit more. I never go to zero carbs, however, because carbohydrates are important for proper body function. This is what I ate for all of my Mr. Olympia victories, and it worked quite well."

Rachel McLish (Pro World Champion, twice Miss Olympia, best-selling author): "Before a competition, the right diet is of utmost importance because the body is so efficient that it will respond immediately to any food you put into it. I feel that diet is as important as training during a precontest cycle. And for one or two weeks before a competition, I feel that diet is easily the most vital factor. Then it can determine whether you win or lose. A month before competing, the training is much more important. Personally, diet isn't very crucial to me in the off-season since I have a fairly fast metabolism."

Lou Ferrigno (Mr. America, Mr. International, twice Mr. Universe, noted film and television actor): "Unlike some of the bigger bodybuilders who consume 300–400 grams of protein per day, I eat only about 150 grams a day. And I'm able to make good gains on this relatively small amount of protein. What I try to do is make sure that my protein comes only from high-quality sources, such as eggs, fish, chicken, and protein supplements.

"Any bodybuilder can make good muscle gains on a half gram—or slightly more—of good-quality protein per pound of body weight. Taking in more protein than that doesn't make you grow any faster. It actually slows down your digestion. Plus, the excess calories can be stored as body fat.

"I don't want you to think, however, that I'm against protein supplements, because I use them often. I mix up a delicious protein shake whenever I'm too rushed to eat a conventional meal or when I want a high-protein, be-tween-meals snack."

Bill Pearl (Mr. America, Mr. USA, four-time Mr. Universe, noted trainer of bodybuilding champions): "Vitamin B complex is definitely associated with tissue growth, as well as with numerous other body functions. Thiamin keeps your nerves healthy and plays a role in proper heart function, riboflavin prevents birth defects, niacin prevents pellagra, B_{12} promotes healthy blood and nerves, folic acid fights anemia, pantothenic acid fights stress, and inositol and choline are essential for fat mobilization in the body.

"In summary, B complex is vitally necessary to your body for reasons other than muscle growth, but particu-larly for muscle growth. It's water-soluble and constantly eliminated from your body in your urine, so it needs to be present in the diet on a daily basis.

"Since B complex is water-soluble, it will be impossible to take too much. Look at the bottle, see what the recom-mended dosage is, and then take twice the amount that's recommended. Be sure, however, to take the B complex capsules periodically throughout the day, one in the morn-ing and again with your evening meal."

Laura Combes (Ms. Florida, first American Women's Body-building Champion, author of *Winning Women's Body-building*): "I start dieting 8–12 weeks before a competition. Precisely when I start depends totally on how much body fat I have to lose. The more fat I've accumulated during the off-season, the longer I'll need to diet before a competition.

"Once I begin my precontest diet, I gradually eliminate more and more foods from my daily menu, and this progressively decreases the calories I consume. Of course, I *could* jump right into a strict dietary regimen, but that would be a tremendous strain on both my mind and body.

"It's easier and healthier to diet sensibly for a long period than to crash diet for a few weeks. Personal experi-ence has taught me that crash dieting is too hard on the mind and body, and it causes you to lose considerable muscle mass."

Casey Viator (Teenage Mr. America, Mr. USA, Mr. America, IFBB Pro Grand Prix Champion, 3rd place in the Mr. Olympia competition): "I don't think that a beginner or intermediate needs to watch his or her diet as much as a professional bodybuilder. Of course, you should avoid junk foods and follow a healthy and balanced diet, but you don't need to be too fanatical about it. I found that milk products helped me enormously when I was on the way up. I also believe in eating red meats when you're growing."

Dr. Lynne Pirie (Superbowl of Bodybuilding Champion): "I keep my diet fairly strict all of the time now, although I certainly didn't do that until just recently. I eat natural foods, and I generally consume fewer than 2,000 calories per day. I can tell instinctively how many calories I consume now, although in the past I had to count every calorie.

"I eat basically white meats, fresh fruits, fresh vegetables, salads, and food supplements. I take a wide variety of supplements but don't ingest that high a dosage of each type of vitamin and mineral. I have been taking a lot of lecithin lately because I think it helps to thin out my skin."

Dale Ruplinger (American and World Middleweight Champion): "I eat baked or broiled chicken breasts without the skin about 365 days a year. I normally have six to eight eggs in the morning with a piece of melon, but close to a competition reduce this to five or six eggs with only one yolk to keep my fats down. Most of the calories in an egg are in the yolk, while the white is essentially pure protein.

"For lunch during my precontest cycle, I have two chicken breasts with a small salad, but I use no salad dressing because of the oil in it. Dinner is basically the same as lunch. I'll also have three or four pieces of low-calorie fruit a day, usually between meals.

"I use a moderate amount of food supplements. I take about 20 dessicated liver tablets per day, 3,000 mg of C, 300 mg each of the B vitamins, and one or two multipacks of vitamins, minerals, and trace elements. Overall, I follow a well-balanced nutritional program both in the off-season and before a contest, which has helped me enormously."

Robby Robinson (Mr. America, Mr. World, Mr. Universe, IFBB Pro Grand Prix Champion): "Dehydrating for a competition releases vital minerals from your system, which causes cramps. Keep your potassium intake up, and you'll have fewer cramps and feel stronger onstage. I personally don't use a diuretic, but I do cut back on water a little. If you cut too much water, however, you'll also lose muscle mass. You may end up looking a little sharper, but you'll also be smaller-looking."

Claudia Wilbourn (Ms. California, runner-up in the World Championships, runner-up Ms. United States, women's bodybuilding pioneer): "Dieting for bodybuilders is hard enough for men. For women, it can be a disastrous experience. The human female naturally carries a great deal more fat than does the male. Her biochemical makeup, with its higher levels of estrogen and other hormones, makes getting extremely lean very difficult. It's even more difficult for women taking estrogen-based oral contraceptives. If you don't know the right way to lower your body fat levels, if you subject your body to unnecessary abuse, the dieting process can be dangerous as well as uncomfortable."

Roger Walker (Heavyweight World Champion): "I take an instinctive approach to precontest diet. Unlike other pro bodybuilders, I don't count calories or the grams of carbohydrate or protein I consume. From the way I look in the mirror and from my energy levels, I can instinctively tell almost exactly what to eat each day. If I'm a touch too smooth two weeks before competing, I'll simply eat less food for two or three days. And conversely, if I'm getting lean too fast, I'll eat more food for a day or two."

Boyer Coe (Teenage Mr. America, Mr. America, three-time Mr. Universe, IFBB Overall Grand Prix Champion): "I used to eat a very high-protein diet with little carbohydrate in it prior to a competition, and I totally neglected to keep track of the amount of fat I was eating. It was steak and eggs, steak and eggs—and for every gram of fat I ate, I was taking in twice the number of calories I would get in a gram of protein or carbohydrate. It's little wonder that I was having trouble getting my body fat level down.

"Then I switched over to a diet in which I kept my protein intake down to about 150–200 grams per day. I ate about 150 grams of carbohydrates each day, but I kept my fat intake absolutely as low as possible. With this type of diet I had an abundance of training energy, enough protein to build muscle, and a sufficiently low caloric intake to reduce my body fat level gradually.

"Combining this type of diet with running really did the trick for me. Running is something that I used to despise, and in the beginning I had to force myself to get out and run every day. But after a month or so I actually began to look forward to it. Now I include running—about three miles per day—in my training program even during the off-season."

Sue Ann McKean (California Champion, Superbowl of Bodybuilding Champion): "I have a very free-flowing, nonmechanical approach to precontest diet. Year-round, I follow a healthy, natural diet. Prior to a competition, I don't count calories, grams of fat, grams of carbohydrate, or grams of protein. I don't even deny myself any of my off-season foods, other than salty foods that might retain excessive water in my body, and then only for the last few days prior to competing. I simply progressively reduce the amount of each food I consume, which automatically decreases my daily caloric consumption. Such a precontest diet is effective, healthy, and easy to follow."

Steve Michalik (Mr. America): "My biggest mistake in bodybuilding was once following a zero-carb diet. I just shriveled up. Now we learn that you need to consume carbohydrates. The luckiest thing I did was to drink a bottle of wine just before a competition. I blew up to my most massive size and had tremendous vascularity as a result. I used this technique for a couple of years after this experience.

"The biggest problem that most people have is believing in the right diet. Even if it worked for them at one competition, for some reason they don't want to do what worked the next time they have a contest. They look for a new gimmick, something they heard about, and it could be detrimental to their onstage appearance."

Mike Mentzer (Mr. America, Mr. Universe, Heavyweight Mr. Olympia, IFBB Pro Grand Prix Champion): "My pre-contest diet is more in tune with the human body's bio-chemistry than are most bodybuilders' dietary programs. By reducing total calories in any diet, a person will lose fat weight. The primary way I reduce my calories for a competition is to cut back drastically on my consumption of fats—no beef, then—and reduce my protein intake to 60 grams per day. Undoubtedly, this sounds incredible to you, but your body does *not* need more than that amount of protein to build big muscles since it is perfectly capable of manufacturing its own protein from other foods.

"The body's preferred source of fuel for energy produc-tion is carbohydrate, so my carbohydrate level is high in order to keep my training energy and daily energy levels up. That's why I can eat ice cream before a competition. As long as I keep my daily caloric intake under a certain level, I get progressively more defined, regardless of what I eat."

Stacey Bentley (Zane Pro Women's Invitational Cham-pion): "I have to start dieting seriously six weeks before a show and semidieting several weeks before that. A tight precontest diet is 800–1,000 calories per day for the last three weeks. This is both low-calorie and low-carbohy-drate, so I get pretty fatigued during the day. As the contest comes close, I fine-tune my calorie intake accord-ing to how I look in the mirror and how far away I am from competing.

"My precontest breakfast is four egg whites and cottage cheese. The egg yolks are high in fat, hence high in calories, so I avoid them prior to a competition. The last two weeks I'll even cut out the cottage cheese at breakfast, since milk products tend to smooth me out. The rest of the day it's fish—basically raw—and a little salad and fruit.

"I'm big on raw fish. I was eating a lot of raw scallops

and raw shark before winning the Zane Pro Invitational. I eat less than a half pound of fish at each meal, however.

"Prior to a competition, I take supplements with every meal, not just with breakfast, as is the case in the off-season. The precontest diet is so tight that I'd probably come up with some sort of nutritional deficiency if I didn't use an extra amount of vitamin and mineral supplements."

Dr. Franco Columbu (Mr. Europe, Mr. Universe, Mr. World, twice Mr. Olympia): "A high-protein diet causes some additional strain on the liver, but you can't call such strain liver *damage*. When you take in excess protein, the body absorbs what it needs and the rest is excreted through the bowels or urine. So you can see that the liver is not very easily damaged by excessive protein intake. If it was, there'd be a lot of dead bodybuilders, since many take in 300–400 grams of protein per day. The liver is damaged far more from the alcohol that some bodybuilders blow out with on Saturday nights. And remember, the absolute worst thing for the liver is drugs, especially oral anabolic steroids."

Hubert Metz (European and World Heavyweight Champion): "My body needs 350–400 grams of protein per day for optimum muscle growth, so I eat at least three meals per day and also take as many as four to six protein drinks. My general diet in the off-season consists primarily of meat, milk products, eggs, vegetables, apples, and food supplements. Before a contest I eat less red meat and more fish and poultry. I also gradually reduce my milk intake, mixing my protein powder with water instead of milk. And I reduce my carbohydrate intake to about 70–80 grams per day. Six to eight weeks of such dieting enables me to reduce my body fat to a minimum."

Dennis Tinerino (Teenage Mr. America, Mr. USA, Mr. North America, Natural Mr. America, Pro and Amateur Mr. Universe): "Food supplements are a must at the Olympian level, as well as for any health-minded individual. I consume a lot of them, say about 200 dessicated liver tablets a day prior to a competition. In the off-season, I still take 50 liver, 2,000 mg of C, B complex, and a full range of other supplements.

Arnold Schwarzenegger: "To be honest, I have won the Mr. Olympia title while taking a lot of supplements, as well as while taking none at all. All of the answers on the subject of supplements are not in. But most of the champions I know take supplements, some massive amounts. So just to be on the safe side, a would-be champion should take supplements. But it's important not to take too much of the fat-soluble vitamins, such as A and D. These vitamins can build up to toxic levels in the body.

"Of course, you must be sure to eat a well-balanced diet, too. Remember, the vitamins you buy in a bottle are only the ones that science has discovered thus far. A lot of what your body needs can be derived only from regular food."

Rachel McLish: "A number of bodybuilders monitor their water balances, but I like to play with mine in the days leading up to a competition. When you are on a low-salt diet all of the time your body will adapt to it and respond in an exaggerated manner by retaining a great deal of water any time you take in a little salt. Having learned this, I ate a ton of salt a week before the last Olympia. I would drink a margarita and eat potato chips and pizza, and I was bloated as a result.

"Because I was bloated with water, no one who saw me a week before I won my second Olympia could believe I was even entering the show. Then, a couple of days before the competition, I monitored my salt intake very closely, and my body released all of the water it had been holding. By tricking my body this way, I ended up looking very tight and muscular."

Boyer Coe: "Resist the postcontest temptation to pig out on junk foods. I know that virtually all body builders overindulge themselves as a reaction to several weeks of strict dieting. But this is a mistake. Some bodybuilders gain as much as 25–30 pounds in the weeks right after a show. Then they have to diet even more strictly for their next contest.

"I keep my body weight within six to eight pounds of contest shape at all times. This way, dieting is never the ordeal for me that it is for many other bodybuilders. And, by dieting sensibly year-round I have more energy to keep my training poundages higher—which allows me to maintain greater muscle mass—than if I had to crash diet prior to a contest.

"You can relax your diet during an off-season cycle and even eat a little of your favorite junk foods occasionally. But your diet should still be healthful and nutritious. You should keep your caloric intake at a level where you can maintain a reasonably low body fat percentage. A nutritious diet should include plenty of protein, fresh vegetables, and natural starches such as rice and potatoes."

Jacques Neuville (World Middleweight Champion): "In general, vitamins and minerals are more efficiently absorbed if they are taken with other foods. Also, you might find that you will become somewhat nauseous if you take vitamin and mineral supplements without other food. If you find it impossible to take supplements throughout the day, at least take them with your breakfast."

Laura Combes: "While I am sure that a vegetarian diet is sufficient for many men and women—including bodybuilders—I build more muscle mass when I eat animal protein. Still, during the off-season I get some protein from my intake of nuts, seeds, grains, seed sprouts, corn, potatoes, and legumes. Such vegetable-source proteins can be eaten if they're consumed in conjunction with animal proteins. The animal protein completes the amino acid balance of vegetable proteins and makes the vegetable proteins more assimilable by the body."

Matt Mendenhall (Runner-up, National Championships): "I feel that a physically active athlete or bodybuilder requires about twice the FDA's recommended daily allowance of one gram of protein per kilogram—2.2 pounds—of body weight. So, I recommend consuming three-fourths to one gram of high-quality protein for every pound of body weight each day. Less protein simply doesn't allow me to build muscle tissue as quickly as I like.

"The highest quality of protein for humans comes from the animal sources, with egg white the most useful type of protein. Red meats like beef and pork are so high in fats that most bodybuilders agree they're of little use in our sport. Poultry, with the fatty skin removed before cooking, and fish are much better protein sources in a bodybuilder's diet. Eggs are also good, especially without the yolks, and you can eat limited milk products in the off-season. Prior to a contest, however, you should avoid milk; an enzyme found in milk retains a great deal of water in your body."

Lori Bowen (USA Champion, National Champion, Pro World Champion): "I go by feel in my diet and don't really know how many calories I eat. During the off-season, I'll eat nothing after five or six in the evening. Twice per day I eat white meat—usually chicken or fish—and plenty of fruit and vegetables. I don't eat much red meat, even though I like it. I also don't eat much junk food, although I do confess that I love Mexican food from time to time during an off-season cycle.

"I have read that a lot of protein is important to a bodybuilder and also that very little is necessary. I fall somewhere in the middle range in actual practice. I follow a high-carbohydrate, low-fat, moderate-protein diet. Complex carbohydrates are the best. My protein intake is between a half and three-quarters of a gram per pound of body weight each day.

"Prior to a competition I might have chicken or fish only every other day. Otherwise I eat all of the green vegetables I want and a moderate amount of fruit, particularly grapefruit. This amounts to less protein than in the off-season, but I've never felt any adverse effects from reducing my protein intake close to a competition."

Charles Glass (American and World Middleweight Champion): "I've seen many potentially great bodybuilders fail to ever win a title due to poor diet discipline. They have great mass, fine symmetry, and essentially perfect proportions but lack the sharp muscularity necessary to win a national or international title. The solution in such a case is to begin a diet earlier—as many as four to six weeks earlier than usual—and it's following a less severe diet that allows more consistent self-discipline. A long, low-intensity diet works wonders for many people who would ordinarily find it difficult to reach peak physical condition."

Lou Ferrigno: "In order to gain solid body weight without resorting to steroid use, I suggest that you begin to eat five or six smaller meals per day, instead of the standard two or three large meals. Smaller meals are more easily digested, and you end up using more of the protein you're eating to build muscle. I'd also suggest that you use a good milk and egg protein supplement.

"Train four days a week on one basic exercise per body part. Do about six sets per muscle group and train as heavily as you can for five to eight reps per set. You should also attempt to cut back on outside physical activities, since all of your physical energies should be channeled into training."

Mohamed Makkawy (Mr. Universe, Mr. International, many times an IFBB Pro Grand Prix Champion): "Sodium is death to a bodybuilder. Whether I am dieting for a competition or not, I never salt my food. And I avoid high-sodium foods such as celery. I also drink eight or nine large glasses of low-sodium water per day, as well as coffee and tea made from low-sodium water.

"I don't drink milk, even in the off-season, because I don't like it. I'll eat a little cheese in the off-season, but not close to a competition because it retains water in the body. Cheese contains a lot of salt.

"I seldom eat junk foods. When I do, it's likely to be a scoop or two of natural ice cream. I can get my calories for the day from ice cream or other junk foods from time to time, but I vastly prefer nutritious foods."

Inger Zetterqvist (European and World Heavyweight Champion): "I believe that training and diet are a 50-50 proposition in the off-season but that diet gains in importance up to a 75-25 ratio during a precontest cycle. I just eat a normal, healthy, balanced diet during the off-season. But I don't overeat, because it's senseless to gain a lot of fat during an off-season phase. Excess body fat simply makes it more difficult to regain contest condition.

"Although I stay in pretty good shape during the off-season, I've discovered that I still need 12 weeks of moderate dieting to reach absolute peak condition. My diet becomes more and more strict as a competition approaches, but it's never less than 1,000 calories per day. Yes, many women diet on as few as 500–600 calories per day, but on less than 1,000 calories I personally don't have enough energy for a decent workout. In other words, if my diet is too strict, I lose muscle mass and quality when preparing for a competition. That's definitely *not* the way to win."

Samir Bannout (Mr. Universe, Mr. World, Mr. Olympia): "In order to win the Olympia in 1983, I was eating only 1,000–1,500 calories per day, and the last 10 days I went on low carbs, less than 30 grams per day. Then I felt and probably looked like a zombie. I was always hungry, even after eating. To win the Olympia, however, I had to pay the price, which was feeling like I was starving. I swear, my stomach must have felt at times like my throat had been cut."

John Terrilli (Mr. Australia, Mr. Australasia, runner-up in the Cesar's Palace Pro Invitational): "During the off-season I eat everything and anything. My mother is a fantastic cook—particularly of Italian dishes—so it's really difficult for me to avoid taking in a lot of calories, even though I'm always careful to consume plenty of good, wholesome food. But just before a competition, my mother changes her meal plans to accommodate me, cooking the fish, chicken, and such that I need to reach peak muscularity.

"I prefer to begin dieting two months before a show, although the point at which I kick in my diet depends on how much body fat I've allowed to accumulate in the off-season. I follow the popular low-fat diet, and the amount of food I consume gradually is reduced, down to as few as 800 calories per day. When my diet is restricted, I'm careful to use more vitamin and mineral supplements. It would be folly to incur a dietary deficiency just before a show."

Dr. Franco Columbu: "My dietary secrets are really very simple but very important. I have a lot of eggs, a lot of fish, a lot of vegetables, a lot of potatoes, and enough fruit to keep my training energy high. That's all there is to it. You'll never make progress on junk food, only on simple, healthy foods as I've described."

Erika Mes (World Lightweight Champion): "In the off-season—other than on Sunday when I eat a little junk food—I consume between 1,500 and 2,000 calories per day. About eight weeks before my competition I will begin to gradually cut calories from my diet. Gradually I eat less and less, until I am down to about 800 calories per day. This consists of green vegetables, broiled fish, and a little low-calorie fruit. Rather than eating actual meals, however, I will nibble a little food all day long, a practice that keeps my waistline small for a show.

"For the World Championships I didn't seem to be cutting up quickly enough, so I took a total fast from food for four days. I drank only water and didn't eat anything. It was not an easy experience, but it did allow me to put myself back on schedule quickly for my peak. Although it wasn't a pleasant experience, I did like the body-cleansing effect of my fast."

Lee Haney (World Heavyweight Champion, Night-of-the-Champions winner, Cesar's Palace Pro Invitational Winner, Mr. Olympia): "I used to start dieting for a competition eight weeks before I was due to peak, and I always ended up peaking two to two-and-a-half weeks too early. In such a case I'd have been a fool not to switch to initiating my diet at the six-week point. This has worked quite well for me ever since."

Albert Beckles (Mr. Universe, Pro Mr. Universe, many

times an IFBB Pro Grand Prix Champion): "My dietary cycle begins with a junk food period. Having deprived myself of such foods for 8–10 weeks before a contest, I need such an indulgence. After about two weeks, however, I sense that I'm beginning to add body fat, so I abruptly halt my junk-out. After that I may have ice cream or some other favorite treat once a week, but no more often than that in the off-season.

"During my off-season cycle, I eat lots of unrefined carbohydrates—fruit, vegetables, rice, potatoes, etc.—because they give me the energy I need for my really heavy workouts. For the type of all-out mass-building training I'm doing during an off-season cycle, I must eat like this.

"Prior to a contest I cut down drastically on my carbohydrate consumption, at times going as close to zero as possible. My diet is also low in fats. This diet makes me somewhat weaker in my workouts, but it allows me to strip off every ounce of body fat."

Matt Mendenhall: "As soon as I discovered that dry popcorn was a great low-calorie snack, I bought an air popper. I love that machine! My favorite popcorn treat is to eat it with Butter Buds and/or Parmesan cheese sprinkled on it."

Arnold Schwarzenegger: "As far as whether or not to eat prior to training is concerned, let me approach this one on two levels—physiologically and according to my own experience.

"Whenever you have food in your stomach, blood is taken out of circulation to aid in digestion. That blood is then not available during exercise. This is why mothers always tell their kids not to go swimming right after a big meal—when the blood supply is down, your muscles can cramp.

"So, it's never a good idea to train on a full stomach. But what about eating just a little? I personally preferred to go to the gym at nine in the morning without eating anything first. It felt to me as if I had more energy this way. Of course, this varies from person to person.

"I would recommend that you don't eat later than two

hours before training, morning or night. And when you do eat, eat lightly. Fruit, for example, gives you energy, but it takes a couple of hours for that energy to get into your system.

"Most of all, avoid eating fats as much as possible before your workouts. It takes many hours for fats to be digested. Therefore, you should not eat them before a workout, only after one."

Mike Christian (California Champion, World Champion): "After years of experimentation, I've found that the best way to override a fast metabolism is to consume small, well-balanced meals frequently throughout the day. I personally eat five to seven times per day, spacing my meals out at regular intervals throughout the day. These smaller meals allow your body to process and utilize the nutrients in a most efficient manner, and this in turn results in an anabolic effect conducive to muscular growth.

"Large meals are digested inefficiently, which in turn interferes with absorption of nutrients. For example, your digestive system can process only about 30 grams of protein each meal and move it into the bloodstream where it can be assimilated into muscle tissue. So, when you consume more than 100 grams of protein at a meal, you're wasting much of what you eat. And you're further clogging up your digestive system, making it less efficient and condemning yourself to digesting even less than 30 grams of protein at a meal. It's a far better practice to eat only 40–50 grams of high-quality protein at each meal.

"You can also move much more protein into your circulatory system by eating more frequently. If you digest and absorb 30 grams per meal, you'll put only 90 grams of protein into your bloodstream with three meals per day. But by eating six times a day, you will digest and absorb twice that amount of protein. So, it makes good sense to eat frequent, small meals each day when attempting to gain muscle mass during an off-season training cycle, doesn't it?"

INDEX